The MONOCLE
Travel Guide Series

Miami

For more information, please visit *gestalten.com*

Bibliographic information published by the Deutsche Nationalbibliothek: The Deutsche Nationalbibliothek lists this publication in the Deutsche National-bibliografie; detailed bibliographic data are available online at *dnb.d-nb.de*

Monocle editor in chief: *Tyler Brûlé*
Monocle editor: *Andrew Tuck*
Guide editor: *Ed Stocker*

Designed by *Monocle*
Proofreading by *Monocle*
Typeset in *Plantin & Helvetica*

Printed by *Offsetdruckerei Grammlich, Pliezhausen*

Made in Germany

Published by *Gestalten*, Berlin 2015
ISBN 978-3-89955-632-2

Welcome
—— Enchantment
awaits

The magic and realism (and the magical realism) of *Miami* are constant themes in this guide. Perhaps more than any other US city – with the notable exception of New York – Miami trades off its *reputation*. But a rep can be a good and a bad thing. For years the Floridian metropolis was seen as a bit of a one-trick pony. Beautiful beaches and *perennial good weather* sure, but also a tad culturally limited and, dare we say it, a little cheesy. The response to this is twofold. First, there is so much more to Miami than *Miami Beach*, actually a separate city from the mainland; failing to get out of this bubble (read: hotel sun lounger) is a big mistake. Second, Miami has changed almost beyond recognition in recent years. And for the better.

This is a city investing heavily in art, design and architecture, both through *international fairs* (Art Basel Miami Beach et al) and venerable museums (a string of enviable *private collections* and the much-lauded Pamm to name a few). Miami is booming and part of the cash influx is being poured into the development of a *sparkling new urban core* (watch this space) in a city that in the past was viewed as a set of distinct suburbs. But money is also being invested in the restoration and maintenance of *historic buildings*, in a country that traditionally has always looked to the new.

The city has a *buzz* that stems from its nascent art and food scenes and its *melting-pot quality*, where the English-speaking and Spanish-speaking Americas collide. Simply put, nowhere in the US looks and feels like Miami. — (M)

Contents
— Navigating
the city

Use the key below to
help navigate the guide
section by section.

(H) Hotels

(F) Food and
drink

(R) Retail

(T) Things
we'd buy

(E) Essays

(C) Culture

(D) Design and
architecture

(S) Sport and
fitness

(W) Walks

012 — 013
Map
Visualise the city with our handy
map of Miami, helping you get to
grips with the key areas covered
in this guide.

014 — 015
Need to know
From everyday etiquette to the
clothing climate, here are some of
the basics for navigating the city's
streets, sights and citizens.

016 — 027
Hotels
Iconic pools, private beaches
and art deco allure: Miami has
a winning mix of splendid and
subtle. Get up to speed on where
to stay for business or pleasure
with our guide to the best stays.

028 — 047
Food and drink
With its coastal location and
Cuban connection, Miami is
suitably imbued with fish and
flavour, as well as playing host to
innovative restaurants and bars
that push the boundaries of taste.
We've singled out the very best.

028 — 041
Restaurants

042 — 043
Local flavour

044 — 047
Drinks

048 — 063
Retail
Laidback or luxury, the city has
an impressive selection of shops
adding colour and cachet to an
already buzzing scene.

048 — 054
Clothing

055 — 056
Concept stores

057 — 058
Home and interior design

059
Shopping centre

060 — 063
Specialist retail

063
Hotel retail

064 — 066
Things we'd buy
Whether you're in the market for
beer and rum or swimsuits and
sunglasses, pick some souvenirs
from our choice selection.

067 — 090
Essays
Miami is a place of contrasts,
which is what draws us to it time
and again. Here, Monocle family
and friends share their passion
for various elements of the city,
revealing where its magic lies.

091 — 103
Culture
See the best of the city with our
guide to galleries, cinemas, music
venues and more.

091 — 092
Cinemas

092 — 093
Theatres

093 — 095
Museums

096
Private collections

097 — 100
Commercial galleries

100 — 102
Music venues

103
Media round-up

104 —— 119
Design and architecture
A dazzling array of styles have thrived (and survived) across Miami. From retro neon signs to Spanish-tiled bus kiosks and geodesic domes, see the city in all its eclectic glory.

104 —— 106
Art deco buildings

107 —— 108
Car parks

109
Mimo buildings

110
Neon Miami

111 —— 114
Miami's alternative styles

114
Street furniture

115 —— 117
Design museums

118 —— 119
Stiltsville

120 —— 127
Sport and fitness
Don't let a city break interrupt your fitness regime. We've put the leg-work into rounding up the finest places in the city to swing a racket, throw a jab or break a sweat.

120 —— 121
Swimming pools

122 —— 123
Water sports/activities

124
Indoor options

124
Tennis

125
Cycling routes

126 —— 127
Running routes

128 —— 137
Walks
One of the best ways to discover a city is by hitting the streets. But where to start? We visit five of the city's most scenic, diverse and architecturally interesting neighbourhoods to highlight enlightening routes through the best that each has to offer.

128 —— 129
Coral Gables

130 —— 131
Design District and Buena Vista

132 —— 133
North Beach

134 —— 135
South Beach

136 —— 137
Wynwood

138 —— 139
Resources
Be in the know with our bite-size guide to the city's events, slang and soundtrack, as well as hints on what will keep you occupied on a rainy day.

140 —— 141
About Monocle
Find out more about our global brand from groundbreaking print, radio, online and film output through to our cafés and shops.

142 —— 143
Acknowledgements
The people who put this guide together: writers, photographers, researchers and all the rest.

144 —— 145
Index

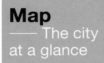

Map
— The city at a glance

Miami-Dade County, essentially incorporating the City of Miami (the mainland) and its neighbourhoods (everywhere from Miami Beach to Coral Gables), used to be a series of mostly residential areas connected by road. This is no longer the case and, while the car is still king, Miami is developing a distinct urban centre that stretches beyond the long-established Downtown into Brickell to the south and the Design District and Mimo to the north.

There's colour, character and diversity almost everywhere you look, from districts that have been settled by émigrés from the Caribbean – Little Havana and Little Haiti being the two most famous examples – to areas that have undergone a distinct regeneration: the aforementioned Design District but also Wynwood and Miami Beach. The trip from one neighbourhood to the next never feels too far so, whether you find yourself in leafy Coral Gables or among the dense skyscrapers of Brickell, it's time to get discovering.

MIAMI INTERNATIONAL AIRPORT

FLORIDA

MID-BEACH

LITTLE HAVANA

SOUTH BEACH

CORAL WAY

COCONUT GROVE   VIRGINIA KEY

LITTLE H

BUENA VIS
DESIGN DIST

De la Cruz Coll
Contemporary Art S

Rubell Family Colle

WYNWO

MIAMI INTERNATIONAL AIRPORT

ALLAPATTAH

Adrienne Arsh
for the Perform

OVERTOWN

DOWNTOW

LITTLE HAVANA

Marlins Park

BRICK

Maximo Gomez Park

CORAL WAY

Coral Gables Museum

Venetian Pool

COCONUT GROVE

Vizcaya Museum and Gardens

Biscayne Bay

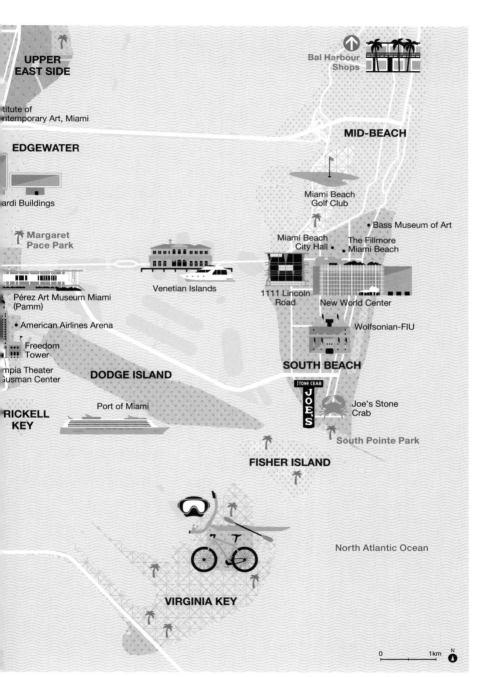

UPPER
EAST SIDE

Bal Harbour
Shops

...titute of
...ntemporary Art, Miami

MID-BEACH

EDGEWATER

...ardi Buildings

Miami Beach
Golf Club

Margaret
Pace Park

• Bass Museum of Art

Miami Beach
City Hall •

The Fillmore
• Miami Beach

Pérez Art Museum Miami
(Pamm)

Venetian Islands

1111 Lincoln
Road

New World Center

• American Airlines Arena

Wolfsonian-FIU

... Freedom
!!! Tower

...mpia Theater
...usman Center

SOUTH BEACH

DODGE ISLAND

STONE CRAB

JOE'S

Joe's Stone
Crab

RICKELL
KEY

Port of Miami

South Pointe Park

FISHER ISLAND

North Atlantic Ocean

VIRGINIA KEY

0   1km N

Need to know
—— Get to grips with the basics

Miami may be one of the most important business cities in the US and an international art hub but it's also a Latin American metropolis with an eclectic cultural heritage. We offer a little advice to help you settle in, from making sure you tip like a Miamian (and don't overpay like a tourist) to talking weather systems with Spanish flair and doing business with a human touch. We've covered everything you need to feel at home in the Magic City – even down to our suggestions on what to wear.

Pay up
Tipping

The standard US rules apply for tipping and that generally means shelling out more than you might in Europe or Asia. The rule of thumb is 15 to 20 per cent in restaurants. However, this being a tourist town, establishments may add the gratuity to the bill for you and then cheekily leave space for an "additional" payment – so make sure you check the paperwork before signing on the dotted line. Remember too that if you're drinking at a bar you'll need to tip around $1 for a beer (slightly more for cocktails) and, this being one of the US's valet-parking capitals, a couple of bucks to the person who moved your car wouldn't go amiss.

I would leave a tip but I'm feeling the pinch at the moment

Drive time
Transport

OK, so you've got the trolley and the Metrorail when it comes to public transport but, unless they're within walking distance of where they need to go, most Miamians rely on their cars. As a visitor, renting one may be a decent option but you'll need to factor in parking costs and actually being able to find a space. The alternative is to get a taxi – but no one in Miami has anything good to say about the ones you hail in the street. The vast majority of the populace instead call an inexpensive service from an app on their mobile phones (you know the ones). Distances are pretty easy but factor in traffic delays – especially at peak times and during Art Basel.

Urban jungle
Nature

Miami's tropical climate and year-round warm weather mean that, as well as admiring all the concrete, steel and aluminium, you should look beyond it to the plants, palms and animals. Don't be surprised if you spot an iguana hanging out on Brickell Key or a zebra longwing butterfly in Coral Gables. They are a reminder that you could consider heading out of town to the swampy, alligator-infused wetlands of the Everglades or, for the less adventurous, Key West.

It's good to talk
Doing business

Here's a tip for those of you who are coming to Miami for business: email isn't always best. It may be the preferred communication for much of the US but in Miami things are a little slower and a little more casual. Maybe it has something to do with the Latin influx or warm climate (or a combination of the two) but Miamians like to have real conversations and that often means you should pick up the phone.

Air navigation
Airports

The nearest hub to the city is Miami International Airport (MIA), 15 minutes' drive from South Beach. It's poorly signed however, so getting to the rental car centre and accessing the MIA Mover (the shuttle to the terminal) isn't the easiest of tasks. As such, visitors should also consider Fort Lauderdale-Hollywood International Airport, 45km (40 to 60 minutes' drive) from Downtown Miami. Several domestic carriers fly here, including JetBlue: a budget airline that nevertheless offers a better service than most of its regular US competitors.

Weather the storm
Climate

Miamians use dates and years to mark time just like the rest of us. But stay here long enough and you'll realise that hurricanes are defining markers. People will often talk about something happening pre- or post- one of these mega-storms; the two most often cited are Betsy (1965) and Andrew (1992). Hurricane season runs from June to November but that's not to say anything catastrophic will happen. In terms of when it's best to visit, November to April is the most pleasant: humidity is at its lowest and temperatures stay in the 20s.

I like to make sure my buried bones are well defended

Sí, hablo español
Language

There's no getting away from the fact that Miami is basically the capital of Latin America. Latinos make up some 70 per cent of the population, the majority from Cuba but also nations as diverse as Guatemala, Venezuela, the Dominican Republic and Colombia. While speaking Spanish isn't essential, you'll constantly hear it during your stay and even a smattering will give you extra insight into the city – and probably get one or two people to smile along the way. Indeed, even non-Spanish speakers use a Latino lexicon (*see page 138*) and knowing your *cortadito* from your *cafecito* (*see essay on page 70*) when choosing a restorative coffee is also important.

Dressed to impress?
Fashion

No one can accuse Miami of being a formal city – that doesn't just go for the way people dress but the way they interact with each other too. With any warm climate you need to be practical and no one will bat an eyelid if you turn up for dinner in shorts and other casual attire. The rules vary greatly depending on where you are and the art-and-graffiti neighbourhood of Wynwood has a very different feel to the more exclusive parts of South Beach (where the shorts may have to go). Things also change around the time of Art Basel Miami Beach, when the influx of New Yorkers brings fashion to the fore. Wherever you end up, hardly anyone does suits.

I'm not allowed to drive anymore but I keep this old thing for the air-con

Cold calculations
Air-conditioning

Hop from car to hotel lobby to restaurant and you will likely be moving from one artificially controlled climate to another. We are, of course, talking about air-conditioning. In the summer months, when the heat and humidity are at their height, you'll be thankful for this respite from the gruelling Miami weather. But some establishments can go a little overboard so it's always wise to pack an extra layer when you head out to eat, in order to avoid getting a chill.

Diverse designs
Architecture

There are few cities that seem to offer such a rich canopy of architectural styles. Who knew that art deco had offshoots such as streamline moderne (or even Depression moderne for that matter)? Or that Mediterranean revival would find such a rich and downright quirky home in Miami? If you're going to truly appreciate this city, make sure you get beyond South Beach's Art Deco District (find out more from page 104).

Hotels
—— Homes away
from home

The sun, the palm trees,
the turquoise colour of the
Atlantic Ocean – and a
ridiculous amount of
choice when it comes
to hotel rooms (some
2,000 to 3,000 are added
each year). The best of
those options are on
Miami Beach: often
art deco mega-hotels
with swimming pools
galore, private beaches,
a handful of restaurants
and just about every
amenity under the sun.
Hunt around and you can
find some decent options
on a smaller scale too.

Even if business or
pleasure take you away
from beach utopia, Miami
feels surprisingly small
and you are never more
than a 20-minute taxi
ride away from the key
mainland neighbourhoods.
Well, except during
traffic-inducing Art Basel.

This *is* Miami so expect
a few little flashy details
that you might not get
in other US cities. And
take advantage of them
– that's what you're here
for, isn't it? Late-night
club? Check. Bowling
alley and ice rink? Check.
Underwater swimming-
pool music? Check.

*How dare
you suggest
I'm overdressed
for the pool*

True to form
Subtle and
precise: The
Raleigh is
timeless

①
The Raleigh, South Beach
Classy affair

Tucked behind tropical plants on
Collins Avenue, the much-loved
Raleigh Hotel has been a cult
favourite since the 1940s. Designed
by famed architect Lawrence Murray
Dixon, the softly detailed hotel has
105 rooms elegantly appointed with
vintage mid-century furnishings.

Unlike many of its neighbours,
the art deco building has a quiet
appeal, from its petite café off the
lobby to its classic Martini Bar and
trademark black-and-white deck
furniture. Everything about this
classic hotel feels authentic, including
its celebrated curved pool, dubbed
the most beautiful in the US by *Life*
magazine in 1947. When you're ready
to get out and explore Miami Beach,
grab one of the hotel's bicycles.
*1775 Collins Avenue, 33139
+1 305 534 6300
raleighhotel.com*

MONOCLE COMMENT: The house-
recommended classic cocktail at
the Martini Bar is the Martinez.

②
Soho Beach House, Mid-Beach
Welcome to the club

Soho Beach House isn't solely for private members, despite being part of the Soho House group – stay here and you get access to the property's ample facilities. Despite the vast lobby, complete with art deco furnishings, there are a modest 50 rooms. Everything oozes good taste.

Lounge in the "screening snug", enjoy the spa with its reclaimed-wood look, eat at one of the three restaurants or head to one of two pools. And the best rooms in the house? Those would be the Beachside 2 corner suites, with views of Miami Beach through two glass-dominated external walls.
4385 Collins Avenue, 33140
+1 786 507 7900
sohobeachhouse.com

MONOCLE COMMENT: We like the little touches at Soho Beach House. The salon/barber area can give you a haircut or a shave, then you can show it off with some fine food (and drink) in the private dining area.

③
The Standard Spa, South Beach
Rest assured

Located on a manmade island on the Venetian Causeway, a few minutes' walk from Miami Beach, this remodelled 1950s property is a fun getaway. The lobby is a mishmash of styles, with Hans Wegner rocking chairs meeting a table-tennis table. And the large outdoor swimming pool has underwater music and is right next to the sea; try the paddle-boarding if you're done lounging.

Many rooms have a nice touch: an outdoor bathtub in which to have a cold soak, a respite from the heat. Decent food at The Lido restaurant, a great shop and a beautiful Turkish hamam make this a relaxing option.
40 Island Avenue, 33139
+1 305 673 1717
standardhotels.com

MONOCLE COMMENT: There's a fine line between staying at a buzzy place and wanting somewhere that offers a retreat. The Standard in Miami manages to straddle that threshold rather nicely.

(4)
Nautilus, South Beach
Smooth sailing

One of the latest properties to debut on Collins Avenue, the Nautilus by Sixty Hotels has been completely regenerated with the help of Miami firm Arquitectonica. Its 1950s frame, designed by one of the most prolific architects of the day in Morris Lapidus, houses 250 well-appointed but unfussy rooms.

The aesthetic draws on the marina with a navy-and-beige colour palette, made markedly more enticing by vintage travel chest inspired minibars. Be sure to pull yourself away to the saltwater pool though, fully equipped with its own bar, or rest on the lawn in Bolivian hammocks overlooking the sea.
1825 Collins Avenue, 33139
+1 305 503 5700
sixtyhotels.com/nautilus

MONOCLE COMMENT: While the signage is a replica, the original green tiles outside have been restored and you'll still find Lapidus's "staircase to nowhere" by the lobby bar.

Finishing touch
—
Attention to detail is key at Nautilus, inside a 1950s building that once housed the Continental South Beach. Look forward to Italian-made bed linen from Sferra and in-room skincare products from Ren for your pampering needs.

Hotel minibars

01 Thompson Miami Beach, Mid-Beach: Teak wood, a terrazzo stone top and antiqued-brass framing make up this art deco-style minibar designed by Martin Brudnizki. The open-style glass shelves showcase a selection of spirits, while the cocktail menu features recipes for classic drinks with a Miami twist – all of which can be made using the impressive provisions from the minibar.
thompsonhotels.com

02 Soho Beach House, Mid-Beach: The "One While Changing" service provides you with a cocktail of your choice mixed by an in-room bartender who wheels a vintage bar cart into your room. The three-tiered dark-wood cart holds a variety of crystalware, drink garnishes and spirits; options include Fluid Dynamics brandy, Don Julio tequila and Fever Tree tonics.
sohobeachhouse.com

03 Hotel Victor, South Beach: Lightly bleached-wood trunk-style minibars act as visual anchors in every room of Hotel Victor. They open to reveal a selection of spirits and snacks – including gourmet delights from Dean & Deluca – and offer ample glass- and tableware.
hotelvictorsouthbeach.com

04 Viceroy Miami, Brickell: Hotel interior designer Kelly Wearstler's modern scheme with an Asian air continues through to the minibar, hidden behind an antique mirrored and brass door. It slides to reveal an espresso machine, spirits and treats including a chocolate-bar library from Vosges Haut-Chocolat.
viceroyhotelsandresorts.com

⑤
Vagabond Hotel, Mimo District
Refreshing memories

Opened in 2014, The Vagabond – a
historic property from the architect
behind the Delano – has been
restored to its 1953 glory with fresh
fun thrown in. There's a nod to mid-
century modern, with furniture by
Stephane Dupoux. But the 45 rooms
have been spruced up with colour
and a tongue-in-cheek lick of kitsch.

The pool is a highlight, with a
restored mosaic mermaid at the
bottom and live music and DJs
in the evenings from Thursday
to Saturday. Also check out the
restaurant from young Angeleno
chef Alex Chang, one of the best
in the city.
7301 Biscayne Boulevard, 33138
+ 1 305 400 8420
thevagabondhotel.com

MONOCLE COMMENT: Get staff to
show you the before-and-after video
of the refurbishment: the derelict
building the owners acquired barely
resembles the sparkling example of
Mimo architecture that it is today.

Step beyond
There are 200 metres of private beach to enjoy

6

1 Hotel South Beach, South Beach
All in one

One of the newest hotels on Miami Beach's Collins Avenue strip, this is a vast property of 426 rooms and 154 residences. The design is contemporary but understated, with off-white walls, ample use of wood and plants and lots of light.

One of the big advantages of 1 Hotel South Beach is the room size, with a standard measuring a whopping 65 sq m. And in case you're wondering about the unusual hue of the wood in the rooms, it's beetle-kill pine. With good pools, several restaurants from chef Tom Colicchio, a spa, gym, boutiques, dog park, gelato bar and café, you've got all your bases covered.
2341 Collins Avenue, 33139
+1 305 604 1000
1hotels.com/south-beach

MONOCLE COMMENT: The bedroom design by New Yorker Meyer Davis is clever, in many rooms filling the space next to the bed with an L-shaped sofa that looks out towards the sea.

My nesting instincts have kicked in, OK?

⑦
The Miami Beach Edition,
Mid-Beach
Alluring addition

Opulent yet sophisticated, The Miami
Beach Edition sits oceanfront in the
middle of Miami Beach. The former
Seville Hotel, cast in white and gold,
evokes a past era of Miami glamour.

Past the lobby's oversized gold
columns and greenery the Market
and Matador restaurants buzz; the
former serves gourmet café options,
the latter Latin cuisine. Rooms are
pristine, elegant and warm. While the
hotel's upper levels and outdoor space
offer an air of sophistication, in the
basement revellers have no shortage
of activities to enjoy: there
is a bowling alley, an ice rink and
a dance floor, of course.
2901 Collins Avenue, 33140
+1 786 257 4500
editionhotels.com

MONOCLE COMMENT: Aside from the
private beach, there are two pools and
a sandy nook shaded by palm trees
where we'd recommend catching an
outdoor film or resting in a hammock.

*I find that one is
never too old to sit
back and admire
the view*

Lush life
—
Plant pots and greenery adorn the hotel

Ⓗ

The Royal Palm South Beach,
South Beach
Mid-century marvel

This hotel was rebuilt and renovated twice in the 2000s, matching its original art deco façade and adding modern towers to house nearly 400 rooms. The interior design is an ode to mid-century modern and the compass rose on the terrazzo lobby floor, green-glass reception desk and porthole windows in the lobby lounge have all been maintained.

Designed by Rottet Studio, rooms are unfussy and smart with a cool Floridian palette. Situated on Collins Avenue, the hotel is a stone's throw from the heart of South Beach but with two spacious pools, direct ocean access and The Florida Cookery restaurant on-site, we understand why you may just want to stay put for a few days.
1545 Collins Avenue, 33139
+1 305 604 5700
royalpalmsouthbeach.com

MONOCLE COMMENT: Developer R Donahue Peebles acquired The Royal Palm South Beach and the adjoining Shorecrest in the late 1990s; the original buildings from the 1930s were demolished soon after as the concrete structures were in a state of disrepair.

Ⓗ

The Delano, South Beach
State of play

With its winged top, this 1940s tower block is one of the finest examples of art deco architecture on South Beach. Rooms are all white with the odd quirk: an apple holder on the wall containing a fresh Granny Smith – with the slogan "An apple a day keeps the doctor away" – and a little angel, also mounted, to watch over guests. You get the sense that designer Philippe Starck is having a bit of fun.
1685 Collins Avenue, 33139
+1 305 672 2000
morganshotelgroup.com

MONOCLE COMMENT: The Delano has one of Miami's best pools and if you're feeling flush, splash out on one of the bungalows that surround it.

Outdoor furniture

01 **Mandarin Oriental, Brickell Key:** Roomy circular chairs made by Frontgate can be found by both the pool and beach. Sink into pastel-coloured cushions – crafted in Miami from sturdy linens – that cover the recliners. Alternatively, lightly sway in one of the nearby hammocks made from off-white natural rope.
mandarinoriental.com

02 **The Palms Hotel & Spa, Mid-Beach:** The lounge chairs that are situated on the tidelines of the private beach or next to the heated swimming pool from Del Tropico are made from a tropical hardwood. The focus on natural materials extends to the pool area cabanas: their palm leaf-thatched roofs are changed every three to five years.
thepalmshotel.com

03 **The Ritz-Carlton, South Beach:** Dark wooden and wicker furniture alongside white-cushioned day beds with metal frames line the pool deck, which overlooks the waters of the Atlantic Ocean. You can upgrade your relaxation and unwind next to the sea in one of the comfortable recliners, which come with matching umbrellas.
ritzcarlton.com

04 **The Setai, South Beach:** Alongside the pool and beach you will find rows of orderly slate-grey lounge-chair cushions, complemented by oak framing. They help to extend and accentuate the art deco Asian-fusion style that was designed by Jean-Michel Gathy and Jaya Ibrahim.
thesetaihotel.com

Casa Tua, South Beach
Bella vita

Miami, rightfully so, is sometimes accused of being a little too brash – everything can seem to be built on an impossibly big scale. But not so at Casa Tua: this is a place that will serve as the perfect antidote to all that bravado.

Casa Tua is all about European subtlety: the name is a nod to Italy and there is no sign outside (all one can deduce is that this is a rather grand Mediterranean revival building with leafy gardens). There are also only five rooms, which are accessed via a spiral external staircase that leads up from a beautiful outdoor terrazzo.
1700 James Avenue, 33139
+1 305 673 0973
casatualifestyle.com/miami

MONOCLE COMMENT: You don't have to be staying here to enjoy the outside patio. Casa Tua's restaurant serves simple Italian dishes, such as spaghetti with clams and zucchini blossoms.

Hide out
This tucked-away gem is a refreshing alternative

11

Mandarin Oriental, Brickell Key
Reliable chain

Whether you're here on business or
you simply want a break from South
Beach, the Mandarin Oriental's
Miami offering is a good option. It
has all you'd expect from the global
brand: impeccable though a little
corporate rooms, a good-sized gym
and the requisite Miami spa.
    Located beside the water on
Brickell Key – a small island just off
the mainland – it's a good spot if
you need to be within easy reach of
the fast-growing business districts
of Brickell and Downtown. It
doesn't have a beach view but you
will be beside the water in sight of
the city's skyscrapers.
500 Brickell Key Drive, 33131
+1 305 913 8288
mandarinoriental.com/miami

MONOCLE COMMENT: One of the
major draws is Peruvian restaurant
La Mar from chef Gastón Acurio,
the man who has pretty much
single-handedly put his nation's
cuisine on the international map.

Urban legend
—
It may lack a
beach but this
spot means
business

And these are
just my outfits
for the spa...

 (12)
The Gale, South Beach
Simple pleasures

The Gale is a little more understated than some of the other Miami Beach mega-hotels. Like other establishments in the area, it harks back to the golden age of art deco, hence the 1940s replica front desk, chandeliers and sconces. One of the nicer touches here is the selection of vintage black-and-white framed photos around the lobby and rooms. Many of them are family portraits of the Galbut family, involved since the hotel's early days when it was actually two hotels: The Gale and The Regent.

The rooms aren't huge – and the hotel could do without stamping its logo on the pillows – but they are comfortable and functional. The rooftop pool sees the sun all day and has one of the best architectural views in the area, gazing at the magnificent icons that are The Delano and The National.
1690 Collins Avenue, 33139
+1 305 673 0199
galehotel.com

MONOCLE COMMENT: The hotel's bar, The Regent Cocktail Club, is a good spot for a sundowner. And if you're in need of a bigger suite, opt to stay at the Kaskades building a block away.

Food and drink
—— The next course

Not long ago the food and drink scene in Miami was deemed good at best; it would have been a bit of a push to call it outstanding. Things, however, have been changing rapidly in the past few years.

Before now, numerous places have tried to be big-venue catch-all restaurants to cater to a wide crowd. Nowadays there is a growing understanding that small can be beautiful, which also means subtler decor, more streamlined, innovative menus and a greater focus on fresh ingredients. From the Spanish-influenced fusion of Klima to the Latino home cooking of 27, top dining in The Magic City has never been better.

What can't you miss? Seafood is a must in Miami, from yellowtail to the sizeable claw of a seasonal stone crab (via the ubiquitous grilled octopus). Then there are the drinks, from the requisite cocktails to the nascent craft-beer scene. And don't forget to sample some Cuban caffeine and hearty, tropics-defying fodder while you're at it too.

Restaurants
Pick of the top tables

① Garcia's, Miami River District
Family-run seafood institution

This place, located on a strip with a string of other fish restaurants, is a Miami favourite that has been serving the catch of the day since 1966. Three generations of the Garcia family, Cuban expats, run the restaurant, which boasts numerous pictures of Havana on the walls to remind them of the motherland. Downstairs has counters for quick-fix meals while upstairs is more expansive, with lots of wood and a few kitsch plastic fish mounted on the wall for good measure.

Don't be scared by the dolphin sandwich on the menu. "It's not Flipper," says manager Luis Garcia. "This is a fish also known as *mahi-mahi*." While there is a brass-tacks element, Garcia's serves the freshest produce (it has its own boats that go out every day) and you should try the fried yellowtail.

398 Northwest North River Drive, 33128
+1 305 375 0765
garciasmiami.com

Keep it reel
——
Garcia's own boats ensure it only serves the best

Catch of the day? Sounds like there might be a 'Fetch' element involved

2

Mandolin, Buena Vista
Mediterranean magic

This small pocket of the Aegean is hidden behind a blue picket fence where the Design District meets the residential neighbourhood of Buena Vista. Mandolin's plant-filled patio and casual deckchair-dining creates the feeling that you've wandered onto a Mediterranean island.

The Greek-Turkish menu is rustic but flavoursome (think *sucuk*, a type of sausage, or calamari with almond tartar dip alongside a straightforward choice of grilled fish and meat skewers), and much of the produce is grown in the attached garden plot. There's also a lovingly assembled selection of items for sale in the on-site Aegean Market, including chilli sauce and Miami-produced honey. And if you're staying at Soho Beach House, the restaurant has a second outpost there.

4312 Northeast 2nd Avenue, 33137
+1 305 749 9140
mandolinmiami.com

Monday blues

Miami's restaurants have a habit of shutting up shop on Mondays (but not Mandolin, in case you're wondering). Make sure you double check opening times if you're heading out to dine at the start of the week.

③

Market at The Miami Beach
Edition, Mid-Beach
Café culture reinvented

Jean-Georges Vongerichten's
Market is one of three restaurants
inside the Edition Hotel. "By
creating multiple outlets of comfort,
culinary and playful experiences,
there's something for everyone,"
says the hotel's Ben Pundole.
 Market sits behind a wall of
plants to the side of the grand
lobby. The open space looks
like a café-marketplace, hence
the name: there is a coffee and juice
bar, a station for charcuterie,
a raw bar and a patisserie. Better
yet, it serves food until 23.00.
2901 Collins Avenue, 33140
+1 786 257 4500
editionhotels.com

Must-try

Flour tortillas with charred
octopus, salsa veracruzana
and pickled jalapeños from
Coyo Taco, Wynwood

There's something very
no-nonsense about the
Mexican-inspired grub that
flies out of Coyo Taco. Service
is brisk and you can choose
from a list of tacos covering
just about every fusion under
the sun. The *carnitas de pato*
(crispy duck) is very good but
it's the *pulpo* (octopus) that's
the winner. We're also fans of
the presentation of the tacos on
racks – now you just have to eat
without spilling down your front.
coyotaco.com

**Upmarket
approach**

Chef Jean-Georges
Vongerichten has a second
restaurant if you're not feeling
the market vibe. Matador
blends influences from Latin
America, the Caribbean
and Spain; try the Peekytoe
crab and corn fritters
with smoked-chilli tartar
sauce.

④

Alter, Wynwood
Praise be

This is the sort of place that is common in a city such as New York but until recently didn't exist in Miami. At Alter, it's all about creating that industrial-chic feel and focusing on exquisitely presented dishes that use locally sourced ingredients.

The menu is colourful, tasteful and unfussy, complemented by a wide-ranging wine list spanning everywhere from the Old World to California and Oregon. Try the young chicken with Valrhona cocoa *molé*, calabaza purée and charred jicama. Undoubtedly Wynwood's standout restaurant.
223 Northwest 23rd Street, 33127
+1 305 573 5996
altermiami.com

⑤

Gigi, Midtown
Night bites

This Midtown spot is best appreciated after a few drinks. The atmosphere is casual and buoyant, staying open most nights until the wee hours. Stop by for simple pan-Asian bites such as a pork steam bun or come hungry and opt for the slightly off-centre udon bolognese.
3470 North Miami Avenue, 33127
+1 305 573 1520
giginow.com

⑥

Makoto, Bal Harbour
Japanese fine dining

From the age of 15, chef Makoto Okuwa cut his culinary teeth in Nagoya under the tutelage of sushi master Shinichi Takegasa, later moving on to the Washington kitchen of Masaharu Morimoto. Now at his second solo project – and eponymous restaurant – Makoto showcases his rapport with traditional *edomae*-sushi techniques by masterfully balancing the flavours with a sprinkling of South Coast flair.

His high-end Japanese menu – which includes miso sea bass and tempura grouper – pairs perfectly with the extensive list of speciality sakés and Japanese craft beers on offer. Located on the luxury-retail strip in Bal Harbour (*see page 59*), the warm dining room extends onto a comfortable terrace, making this a popular pit-stop for the area's ravenous shoppers.
9700 Collins Avenue, 33154
+1 305 864 8600
makoto-restaurant.com

Juice bars

01 El Palacio de los Jugos, citywide: An institution in Miami for more than 35 years – since Cuban Americans Apolonia and Reinaldo Bermudez opened it as a small fruit store, in fact. Now with multiple locations around Miami, this is a winning refuge for fresh juices and coconuts. It's to-the-point and unashamedly Latino.
elpalaciodelosjugos.com

02 Ten Fruits, Downtown: Peruvian-born Alexander Vasquez founded Ten Fruits to bring a taste of his childhood – the organic tropical fruits, nuts and roots from the Amazon – to Miami. That influence is also found in tasty açaí bowls and salads packed with South American goodness.
tenfruits.com

03 Jucy Lu, Wynwood: This Venezuelan-inspired spot has a long list of delicious cold-pressed juices in nearly every colour of the rainbow. There's also a selection of raw, vegan and gluten-free snacks.
jucylu.com

04 Jugofresh, citywide: This Miami favourite can be found throughout the city. The cold-pressed juice combinations are the creations of classically trained chef Darren Laszlo. The atmosphere is pretty fun too.
jugofresh.com

05 Sunset Juice Café, Sunset Harbour: This neighbourhood café offers a full-service kitchen, ideal when you want to pair your green juice with a bright salad.
sunsetjuicecafe.com

Ice cream

01 Azucar, Little Havana:
Located on the main
Calle Ocho strip in Little
Havana, you can't really
miss this one thanks to
the gigantic ice cream
cone (fake, worry not)
– complete with five
impressively generous
scoops – attached to the
shop's façade. This may
not be the best-looking
place in the world but its
handmade offerings hit
the sweet spot. Try the
plátano maduro (sweet
plantain) or café con
leche flavours.
azucaricecream.com

02 Lulu's, Edgewater: That
isn't smoke rising from
the counter as you walk
in: it's the nitrogen used
to freeze the ice cream.
Why? We're told that
it makes the finished
product much smoother
because there are fewer
ice crystals. Whatever
Lulu's is doing, it's
working pretty well; refuse
the Nutella flavour at your
peril. Everything here is
fresh and seasonal and
you can add toppings
such as waffle bits or
sliced almonds to your
splendid scoops.
lulus-icecream.com

03 Bianco Gelato, Coconut
Grove: A simple,
beautifully designed,
space, Bianco Gelato
opened in 2014 selling
organic ice cream with
tempting flavours such
as pear, cookies and
cream or peanut butter
and salt caramel. This
place caters to a broad
church, with vegan options
and brownies, muffins
and coffee for something
different; there's also
a fridge packed full of
popsicles.
biancogelato.com

⑦
Harry's Pizzeria, Design District
Pie in the sky

The curved neon sign outside
announces this restaurant's intent
with a simple word: "Pizza". It
pretty much sums up the ethos of
this firm favourite, established in
2011. The uncomplicated menu
and focus on fresh ingredients
makes for a winning combination.

Toppings are inventive (braised
fennel, or short rib with cave-aged
gruyère, perhaps?) and there are
also daily specials for those who
wish to sidestep the dough. Add
a decent wine list, a rather good
panna cotta and coffee from roaster
Panther and you're in business.
3918 North Miami Avenue, 33127
+1 786 275 4963
harryspizzeria.com

⑧
Vagabond Restaurant,
Mimo District
Artful blend

This hip, art-centric restaurant
sits next to the revived Vagabond
Hotel, and serves a global medley
of dishes from young chef Alex
Chang (*pictured*). In partnership
with restaurateur and art collector
Alvaro Perez Miranda, Chang's
menu draws on his experience in
kitchens across California, Mexico,
Belgium and Japan.

The food is inspired and
mature. We rather like the rabbit
legs in jungle curry with fermented
chard when it features on the
seasonal menu.
7301 Biscayne Boulevard, 33138
+1 786 409 5635
vagabondrestaurant.com

Slow down
—
Relax with
an 'on Miami
time' cocktail
at the bar

⑨
Joe's Stone Crab, South Beach
Shell out

If your trip coincides with the stone-crab season (15 October to 15 May), there's simply no skipping the century-old institution Joe's Stone Crab. Harvested from the Florida Panhandle to Key West, this specific breed of stone crab is sweet and tender – much like a lobster – and is best boiled then served cold with a generous dollop of Joe's mustard sauce. Don't be alarmed when your order arrives as a mountain of claws: fishermen are only allowed to harvest the crab's one oversized claw, releasing the animal to then regenerate its missing limb (which it can do three to four times).

Joe's maintains a strict no-booking policy, so head over for a long lunch or endure the dinner wait from your perch at the bar while watching members of Miami's top drawer saunter through the dining hall.
11 Washington Avenue, 33139
+1 305 673 0365
joesstonecrab.com

Claw materials
———
Pioneers on the Miami restaurant scene, Joe and Jennie Weiss were the first to serve the then little-known stone crab, which over four generations has fed the likes of Frank Sinatra, Muhammad Ali and, more recently, President Obama.

Blue Collar, Mimo District
Take comfort

Blue Collar – owned by Daniel Serfer, the man behind the equally popular oyster bar Mignonette – serves genuine American fare, or what staff call "food that people like to eat".

This small, unassuming venue has an extensive menu that focuses on meat-heavy comfort fodder. There's a vast brunch selection, including eggs benedict with pulled pork that's not for the faint-hearted, alongside lunch and dinner options that delve into a pleasing selection of burgers, ribs, braised dishes and grilled fish. For lighter eaters, there's a blackboard above the open kitchen counter announcing everything from grilled asparagus and caramelised Brussels sprouts to roasted Yukon Gold potatoes and sautéed kale (alongside the meaty dailies, of course).
6730 Biscayne Boulevard, 33138
+1 305 756 0366
bluecollarmiami.com

Michael's Genuine, Design District
Beyond a bistro

Tucked away in the Design District's Atlas Plaza is a beacon for no-frills food: Michael's Genuine. Opened in 2007, Michael Schwartz's bistro grows and serves flavoursome food in an airy setting.

Although the menu is seasonal, don't miss the pork belly should it appear as a special. Whatever you choose, it's best washed down with American Ale: the restaurant's home brew. If you want to recreate the taste experience, pick up Schwartz's *Down to Earth Cooking for People Who Love to Eat* as you roll out.
130 Northeast 40th Street, 33137
+1 305 573 5550
michaelsgenuine.com

Tap to the beat
—
Enjoy Haitian jazz-folk while you dine

Tap Tap, South Beach
Hooked on Haiti

You should come to this vibrant Haitian establishment perched on the southern end of South Beach for the atmosphere alone: inside the lone grey building, brightly frescoed walls and multi-coloured decor are strikingly merry.

The fare is casual: think stews served with rice and plantain, simply plated. The malanga fritters, shrimp in coconut sauce and the half chicken are not to be missed. This quirky spot is tried and true: Katherine Kean, a documentary film-maker, opened it in 1994 to promote Haiti's art, culture and food.

819 5th Street, 33139
+1 305 672 2898
taptapmiamibeach.com

Coffee shops

01 **Panther, Wynwood:**
All roasted in small quantities on-site, Panther Coffee is Miami's undisputed number one. Joel and Leticia Pollock personally source all of their beans, making the most of longstanding relationships with coffee producers throughout the world and their two decades of experience in roasting. Outlets are all over town now, but the Wynwood venue is the best.
panthercoffee.com

02 **Threefold, Coral Gables:**
Aussie owners Teresa and Nick Sharp bring a taste from Down Under to Miami with this all-day breakfast joint. Threefold blends Melbourne's coffee philosophy (using Panther-roasted beans) with the fresh produce of south Florida in this comfy, modern café. Stop here for a flat white as it should be.
threefoldcafe.com

03 **Mister Block, Wynwood:**
Opened in 2015, this crisp café offers an alternative to Panther should you be seeking one. Mister Block serves Counter Culture coffee, sweet and savoury pastries and pantry items such as nut butters from Big Spoon Roasters. There's outdoor seating in the back if the nearby shopping scene has worn you out.
misterblockcafe.com

How else do you think we stay awake all night?

13
Naoe, Brickell Key
Sushi to savour

Chef Kevin Cory (*pictured*) and manager Wendy Maharlika fought an uphill battle to establish Japanese restaurant Naoe. Opening it in 2009 amid a volatile economic climate, the pair originally juggled outside jobs while operating the restaurant, only to lose their former Sunny Isles Beach tenancy. "We'd wash dishes until sunrise; afterwards I'd take the laundry to do at home, rest, then drive around for groceries," says Cory.

Fast-forward to the present and the *omakase* (chef-selected) menu and impressive range of saké from the Cory family's Japan-based Nakamura Brewery has garnered Naoe a reputation as one of the best sushi restaurants in Florida. Bookings are taken well in advance for both Naoe and its communal dining alternative N by Naoe located next door.
661 Brickell Key Drive, 33131
+1 305 947 6263
naoemiami.com

14
La Mar, Brickell
Presenting Peru

It's an utter mystery why La Mar – a Peruvian restaurant from the country's star chef Gastón Acurio – failed in New York. Maybe it had something to do with the 5th Avenue location; whatever the reason, the Miami outpost inside the Mandarin Oriental is suffering no such problems.

The clientele is largely Latin and the food is delicate and delicious. There's a dedicated ceviche bar and a particularly good set-lunch menu, not least the *fideos machos*: squid-ink pasta with the catch of the day.
500 Brickell Key Drive, 33131
+1 305 913 8358
mandarinoriental.com

27, Mid-Beach
Beautifully balanced

There are plenty of restaurants filled with flash in Miami; 27 is the exact opposite. Set inside a historic house, the atmosphere – thanks to the design by Roman and Williams – is inviting and unpretentious, with eclectic furniture and mismatched dishes. Despite the casual feel, the food and cocktails are world-class, with a menu that mixes Jewish and Latin flavours.

Everything on the menu is delightful but you can't go wrong with the day's catch in coconut curry and the winning tahini-kale salad with crispy chickpeas.
2727 Indian Creek Drive, 33140
+ 1 305 531 2727
thefreehand.com

The notion of eating like a bird just got redefined

⑯
Klima, Mid-Beach
Simply Spain

Opened in March 2015, Klima
has quickly become a trusted
venue for well-executed Spanish
fare in a comfortable, ultra-
modern environment. The 70-seat
restaurant sits discreetly near
Collins Avenue on 23rd Street,
plant-filled and subtly designed.

Executive chef David Rustarazo
brings a contemporary play on
cuisine from Barcelona, reflecting
the roots of Klima's founders Pablo
Fernández-Valdés and Yago Giner.
The food is presented beautifully
so you may not want to take a
bite. But do; the bursting flavours
will make you exceedingly happy
that you tucked in. The fennel,
burrata and Kalamata olives with
sun-dried tomato, as well as the half-
cooked egg-and-potato parmentier
with Iberian ham, are bona fide
showstoppers.
210 23rd Street, 33139
+1 786 453 2779
klimamiami.com

Bakeries

**01 Buena Vista Deli,
Buena Vista:** Bread at
this charming dine-in
pastry shop is prepared
in the French style
every morning. Grab
a perfect loaf to go
or sit with a Cuban
coffee and a peach-tart
bourdaloue. The deli also
functions as a laidback
and pretty good value
restaurant. The die-hard
neighbourhood patronage
means there's great
people-watching, too.
buenavistadeli.com

**02 Zak The Baker,
Wynwood:** Started in Zak
Stern's garage in 2012,
today this establishment
bakes Miami's favourite
loaf. Beyond this classic
sourdough, Zak The
Baker makes beautiful
tartines, pastries and
cakes, as well as soups
and salads. Honey-butter
toast or farmer's cheese
with caramelised onion,
perhaps? A must-visit.
zakthebaker.com

**03 True Loaf, Sunset
Harbour:** Tomas
Strulovic serves classic,
perfect-looking bread
and pastries with an
occasional twist. The
sourdough is excellent
and the croissants can
stand up and be counted
with their French-made
counterparts. But it's the
mango-and-herb focaccia
that is truly special.
+1 786 216 7207

*Why do
ducks get to
monopolise
the bread-
eating scene?*

High flyer
Colicchio has restaurants from NYC to Las Vegas

17
Beachcraft, Mid-Beach
Welcome breeze

Although this is a hotel restaurant, the soft-wooded space, peppered with accents of caramel leather and stone detailing, feels like a seaside cottage thanks to the design by New York's Meyer Davis Studio.

The menu is the handiwork of renowned chef Tom Colicchio and, like the ambience, his food is fresh and straightforward. The cuisine leans towards the Mediterranean complemented by nods to its south Florida location. Don't overlook the sea urchin and peekytoe-crab bucatini or sea-scallop ceviche with currants and pink peppercorns.
2395 Collins Avenue, 31339
+1 305 604 6700
craftrestaurantsinc.com

The name game

Fooq's is in the evolving zone known as the Arts & Entertainment District, a parcel of land connecting Wynwood, the Design District and Downtown. The rebranding of the area as a nightlife hotspot is an attempt to put a once-overlooked 'hood on the map.

Must-try

Key-lime pie from Fireman Derek's Bake Shop and Café, Wynwood
There's a beauty in the simplicity of this dish in that it does exactly what you would expect: provide a zesty, sugary pudding punch. And although this pie may be ubiquitous in Florida (key limes are from the Sunshine State after all) this is the best we've had. Fireman Derek's Bake Shop – founded in 1983 – is run by an actual City of Miami fireman called, you guessed it, Derek. The man likes to bake during his time off.
firemanderekspies.com

⑱
Fooq's, Downtown
Homeward bound

With everything seemingly built on a large scale in Miami, it's great to find a place that is two things: firstly, diminutive (well, by Miami standards anyway) and secondly, well and truly a neighbourhood joint. The latter probably has something to do with the area: not long ago northern Downtown was a no-go but is now solidly up-and-coming.

Owner David Foulquier, a New Yorker, is passionate about the menu, especially the wine: he imports rare bottles from the Old World that don't make it to the city's other establishments. The food is excellent and nods to his French and Iranian heritage, with dishes such as Persian-peach chicken and croissant bread pudding, alongside American staples. And how does he classify it? "Locally sourced, home-style, international comfort food."
1035 North Miami Avenue, 33136
+1 786 536 2749
fooqsmiami.com

⑳ Casa Tua, South Beach
Taste of Italy

Arriving here feels a bit like being let in on a secret: there's no signage as you enter and the impressive Mediterranean-style mansion is nestled among some serious foliage. There are a handful of beautiful rooms to stay in but taking a pew on the patio isn't too shabby either.

The food is simple (risotto primavera, say, or tuna tartare) but delicious. "Casa Tua is more than a restaurant: basically, it's a home," says owner Miky Grendene. "Our dishes are inspired by the authentic northern Italian cuisine that I grew up with."
1700 James Avenue, 33139
+ 1 305 673 1010
casatualifestyle.com

VIP service
Casa Tua club members enjoy special events and perks

⑲ Drunken Dragon, South Beach
Midnight meals

If you're enjoying traipsing the bars of South Beach and in need of a late-night refuel, look out for the red-neon "Market" sign signalling Drunken Dragon. Don't be deterred by its fast-food neighbours: this lively Korean BBQ-cum-tiki-bar dishes up great Korean fusion plates to share.

Midnight favourites include spicy pork Kurobuta Dog and the twice-fried chicken wings. For something a little more filling, opt for a table with a communal grill and order a selection of marinated meats and vegetables that will be cooked to your liking.
1424 Alton Road, 33139
+ 1 305 397 8556
drunkendragon.com

You can shee two palm treesh over there too, right?

Local flavour
Taste of Cuba

Mixing it up — In Tampa, they add salami to a 'Cubano'

① David's, South Beach
Fit to burst

One of the most established Cuban cafés in Miami, David's has seen plenty of changes since it was founded in 1977. Indeed, back then South Beach was a very different place. Recently relocated, it still has the same low-key vibe and food. The Cuban sandwich (also known as a *Cubano*) is particularly good: ham, pork, Swiss cheese, pickles and mustard. Or mix things up and go for the *medianoche* (the same ingredients as above but on bright-yellow *pan dulce*). Also try the *batido de mamey*: a juice made from a native Cuban fruit.
919 Alton Road, 33139
+1 305 534 8736
davidscafe.com

②
Enriqueta's, Wynwood
Regular fixture

There is nothing fancy about
Enriqueta's but that's the point
when it comes to Miami's best
Cuban establishments. The tables
and chairs are simple metal-framed
numbers and there are stools up
around the bar.

The menu is made up of
hearty Cuban food: everything
from *vaca frita* (fried cow) – strips
of beef served with rice, beans and
plantain – to the requisite Cuban
sandwiches (one of the most
popular takeaway items on the
menu) via coffee and juices,
all served on a kitsch Florida
paper place mat.
186 Northeast 29th Street, 33137
+1 305 573 4681

③
Versailles Restaurant, Little Havana
Grand designs

Why would an authentic Cuban
restaurant be named after a French
17th-century palace? Well, dating
back to 1971, the restaurant and
adjoining bakery-cum-café's palatial
façade is adorned with mosaics and
its dining room resembles the Hall
of Mirrors, complete with
a series of opulent chandeliers.

A neon sign outside boasts
"The World's Most Famous
Cuban Restaurant" and it is Little
Havana's ultimate neighbourhood
joint. Order an oven-fresh guava-
cheese *pastelito* and a *cortadito*
coffee for a taste of the motherland.
3555 Southwest 8th Street, 33135
+1 305 444 0240
versaillesrestaurant.com

Drinks
The best mix

① Martini Bar at The Raleigh,
South Beach
Great escape

This is a classic: a venerable
spot secluded from the lobby of
the hotel that has been pouring
cocktails for more than 70 years.

A handful of red stools face
the art deco bar, where you'll
find Nash Pacariz mixing drinks.
He will take nearly any cocktail
requests but he recommends
The Martinez: older than the
Martini, it has gin with sweet
vermouth and maraschino.
"It's fresh and you can drink
it all day," he says. Who are
we to argue?
1775 Collins Avenue, 33139
+1 305 534 6300
raleighhotel.com

*I like to make
sure I drink in the
atmosphere – this
is my fourth*

② The Regent Cocktail Club,
South Beach
Past masters

Set inside The Gale Hotel, The
Regent Cocktail Club truly lives
up to its name. The bar is loyal
to the year that it opened (1941),
featuring bartenders dressed in
waistcoats mixing cocktails with
egg whites, live music and cigar
smoking on the balcony.

Evenings are vibrant: flamenco
dancing every Monday and live
Cuban music on Wednesdays. Also,
if your timing is right, you can catch
the twice-monthly "fundamentals
of bartending" course, which is
open to the public.
1690 Collins Avenue, 33139
+1 786 975 2555
galehotel.com

③
The Broken Shaker at the
Freehand, Mid-Beach
Causing a stir

It's not typical that a bar set inside
a hostel is nominated for a James
Beard award (a top US culinary
prize) but The Broken Shaker has
received high praise ever since it
opened. The concept and bar
programme is the handiwork of
partners Elad Zvi and Gabriel
Orta. The duo use herbs and spices
from the on-site garden and freshly
pressed ingredients to make
homemade syrups and sodas.

The menu has been known to
change but these skilled drink-
makers will happily fashion
something to order (assuming the
bar isn't too packed). The indoor
area houses only a few seats but the
patio has plenty of deck furniture
for you to enjoy the evening air or
check out the pretty young things
who frequent this relaxed Miami
Beach cocktail spot.
2727 Indian Creek Drive, 33140
+ 1 786 325 8974
thefreehand.com

**Hostel
hospitality**
——
We're slightly surprised
to be recommending a bar
inside a hostel – but this isn't
your average auberge. Instead,
it's a colourful, fun and
tasteful take on a hostel that
extends to everything around
it, including the excellent 27
restaurant. These people can
do no wrong.

Hip but humble
——
Having a
drink here is
refreshingly
low-key

(4)
Ball & Chain, Little Havana
Stage right

This famed bar and music venue
originally opened its doors in
1935 and was a staple of Miami's
nightlife scene for two decades
before falling by the wayside.
In its heyday, performers such as
Billie Holiday, Count Basie and
Chet Baker took to the stage.
　Reopened in 2014 by Bill Fuller
and partners Zack and Ben Bush,
the space pays homage to its history
with deep-green walls, leafed fans
along the wooden ceiling beams
and a colourfully panelled central
bar. The expansive space leads out
to its even larger patio.
1513 Southwest 8th Street, 33135
+1 305 643 7820
ballandchainmiami.com

Sorry, cocktails seem to have this effect on me

Magic number

Ball & Chain is located on
8th Street – but the address
tends to go by its Spanish
name (Calle Ocho) due to
its location in Little Havana.
Although this strip is a bit of
a tourist trap, it offers a slice
of island life through its
cigar shops and people
playing draughts.

(5)
Gramps, Wynwood
Respect your elders

Gramps, founded by Miami
resident Adam Gersten, became
an immediate hit when it opened
in 2012. Gersten's vision is far
from the glitz of South Beach:
the relaxed watering hole looks
like an oversized dive with its sparse
interior but it has excellent cocktails
and a welcoming attitude.
　The laidback outdoor space is
a gem too, filled with palm trees,
strung lights and picnic tables;
there's often live music and, from
time to time, karaoke, "Nerd Nite"
lectures and even alligator-wrestling.
A good spirit is encouraged.
176 Northwest 24th Street, 33127
+1 305 699 2669
gramps.com

(6)
Boxelder, Wynwood
Brew ha-ha

This haunt has one of the top beer selections in the city, with 20 taps of primarily Floridian brews as well as an epic selection of bottles from around the world. "Miami got its first micro-brewery just a few years ago," says co-owner Nicole Darnell. "Now they're taking off."

Nicole founded Boxelder with her husband Adam after the two gave up city life in New York. They keep a cosy atmosphere within the walls of their industrial space, where they can typically be found behind the bar.

2825 Northwest 2nd Avenue
Unit C, 33127
+1 305 942 7769
bxldr.com

Breweries

01 **Concrete Beach Brewery, Wynwood:**
This is one of a few microbreweries that have sprung up in Wynwood in the past few years, and we're big fans of the company's fun, colourful branding. The beer isn't too shabby either; try the Stiltsville Pilsner (which has a hoppy kick) or the Rica IPA on tap at the brewery's 'Social Hall'. As at the other beer-makers nearby, you can also get weekend tours of the factory.
concretebeach brewery.com

02 **Wynwood Brewing Company, Wynwood:**
This was the first craft brewery to open up in the neighbourhood in 2011. Wynwood Brewing Company normally has four core beers on tap made on-site, as well as a host of visiting brews, mostly from Florida. It also organises tours at the weekend for $10. And hey, you get a free pint glass thrown in for your "cultural" efforts.
wynwoodbrewing.com

03 **MIA Brewing Co, Doral:**
There's something very Miami about the bright blue, yellow and pink of MIA's logo; we can't quite decide if we love it or hate it. But we have no such doubts about the excellent beers, some of which have great names such as the Belgian-inspired Tourist Trappe. MIA also has an epic amount of guest beer and small-plate pub grub that it refers to, rather optimistically, as "tapas".
miabrewing.com

Retail
—— Treats
in store

Miami's south Floridian culture combines with its Latin influence to permeate everything about this one-of-a-kind city – and that extends to retail. There are plenty of beach-life Brazilian paddles to choose from – or breezy linens, woven sandals and casual totes for that matter.

But beyond the obvious warm-weather accessories there are also shops catering to the international clientele of this sunshine town. You can find the world's luxury brands housed in retail hubs such as Bal Harbour and the Design District. Adding to the mix are shops that bring a cosmopolitan flair to Miami by importing cult-favourite brands from New York, Paris, Tokyo and Sydney.

So whether you want something to shine in at night or an outfit in which to saunter onto the beach, step this way.

Down to earth
—
There's also
a ground-level
Alchemist at
1103

①
Alchemist, South Beach
Clearly cutting edge

Housed on the fifth floor of the
eye-catching multi-storey car park
designed by Swiss architecture firm
Herzog & de Meuron (*see page
108*), Alchemist is a fashion retailer
that is just as edgy as its location.

This glass box of goodies set
amid stark concrete was opened
by husband-and-wife team Roma
and Erika Cohen in 2010 and
sports floor-to-ceiling windows that
flood the retail space with light.
The bright, open design helps to
show off the Cohens' selection of
brands that include favourites such
as Comme des Garçons, Junya
Watanabe and Rick Owens.

The pair have also opened two
other locations in Miami, including
a jewellery boutique in the city's
Design District. "Our shops have
an ultra-modern and timeless feel
while maintaining a distinctive
sense of luxury," says Roma.
*1111 Lincoln Road, 33139
+1 305 531 4653
shopalchemist.com*

②
Atrium, South Beach
Big Apple goes south

Founded by Sam Ben-Avraham
in 2007, this import from New
York boasts a wide-open space and
stocks fine merchandise for both
men and women.

Peruse the shelves for a selection
from Phillip Lim, Comme des
Garçons, Rag & Bone and Opening
Ceremony, as well as footwear by
the likes of Alexander McQueen
and Giuseppe Zanotti. Standing
out from its big brother to the
north, Atrium also carries a first-
rate selection of swimwear from
brands such as Onia, Orlebar
Brown and Mikoh.
*1931 Collins Avenue, 33139
+1 305 695 0757
atriumnyc.com*

③
Loewe, Design District
Bags of style

Madrid-based fashion house Loewe
has made a name for itself around
the world with its exquisitely
crafted leather goods and range of
men's and womenswear. Now it has
its first North American outlet, and
it's in Miami's Design District.

To celebrate the occasion,
creative director Jonathan Anderson
has designed a remarkable shop in
which the central area is dominated
by an 18th-century *hórreo*, a
wooden granary once commonly
found in large farmhouses across
the Iberian peninsula; it's quite a
statement of identity.

High ceilings and atmospheric
lighting showcase the historical
bridge-like structure within this
contemporary space, next to
which Loewe's classic Amazona
and Flamenco Madrid-made
leather bags and Anderson's latest
collections sit like works of art.
*110 Northeast 39th Street, 33137
+1 305 576 7601
loewe.com*

④
Coltorti, South Beach
A little Italy

Italian fashion expert Coltorti first
opened its doors to the US market
in Miami in 2010. The shop is on
the ground floor of a concrete car
park-cum-architectural wonder (*see
page 108*), where white interiors
offset by sculptural gold and acrylic
displays play host to some of Italy's
most prominent labels.

From Valentino's latest and
Sergio Rossi's bags and shoes to the
vivacious prints of 28.5, director
Johnny Alvarez de la Cruz ensures
that the boldest looks make it from
the streets of Italy to the tropical
climes of Miami Beach.
1111 Lincoln Road, 33139
+1 786 517 1330
coltortimiami.com

> Not only
> do I look
> great but
> I can also
> hide from
> mean cats

⑤
Base, South Beach
No-nonsense menswear

Base's flagship, founded in 1989,
is the definition of a well-executed
concept store. Hidden from view
just off what has become an
overrun stretch of retail outlets on
Lincoln Road, it has literally set
itself apart.

Creative director Steven Giles
stocks clothing from Norse Projects
and Zanerobe, watches by Nixon
and an in-house line of fragrances.
The utilitarian shop fixtures are
largely mobile so the layout of
vinyl, books, grooming supplies,
footwear and accessories shift
depending on emphasis.
927 Lincoln Road, 33139
+1 305 531 4982
baseworld.com

⑥
The Webster, South Beach
Chic temple

For fashion lovers, walking into this
soft-pink art deco boutique may
feel like a religious experience. The
oversized shop lines its three floors
with more than 95 top brands,
including Celine, Acne Studios,
Maison Kitsuné, Visvim and
Opening Ceremony, accompanied
by a choice selection of magazines.

Conceived by Laure Hériard
Dubreuil, The Webster has recently
expanded with two new locations,
including a menswear-only shop
in Bal Harbour, but this 1939
Henry Hohauser structure is still
our favourite.
1220 Collins Avenue, 33139
+1 305 674 7899
thewebstermiami.com

⑦
Curve, South Beach
High-end womenswear

Women's clothing retailer Curve
is one of a family of boutiques
founded by Nevena Borissova; she
opened her first in Los Angeles in
1997 with the goal of discovering
and promoting new design talent.

The chic owner continues to act
as head buyer for her five shops,
which carry top-of-the-market
brands. At the Miami location
you'll find labels such as Alexander
Wang, Oliver Peoples, Acne and
Anndra Neen. Many of the staff
are experienced former stylists so
don't be too shy about asking for
their advice.
2000 Collins Avenue, 33139
+1 305 532 6722
shopcurve.com

Bouncing back
—
Mimo's Biscayne Boulevard
is experiencing a revival
that's returning the strip to
the vibrant hub it once was.
Renovations will transform
the art deco Shrine Building
into retail space, while the
proposed Biscayne Green will
provide the area with much-
needed parkland.

⑧
Hint, Mimo District
Well-kept secret

This chic destination is a bit of an
anomaly in an area set to continue
developing over the next few
years. Limited-edition and one-off
couture pieces as well as casual
womenswear and hard-to-find
accessories are selected by store
owner Mariella Gonzalez, who
opened this boutique in 2013.

Notable and new names such as
Smythe, Marie Sainte Pierre, Ivan
Grundahl and Viviana Uchitel are
all here but the accessories alone
are a draw: sculptural magnifying
glass, horse-hair necklace or art
deco coffee set, anyone?
6301 Biscayne Boulevard, 33138
+1 786 518 2715
hintmiami.com

9

OFY, Downtown
Smart but low-key menswear

Third-generation menswear purveyor Ofir Farahan established OFY, specialising in smart-casual designs, in 2013. The shop stocks knitwear and jackets from US designers such as Todd Snyder and Matiere, and sunglasses and trunks from brands including Illesteva and Onia.

The collection will take you from beach to town with ease. OFY appeals to the urbanites of Miami with its sharp but effortless garments, Downtown location smack in the middle of Brickell Village and Stella Artois in the fridge.
900 South Miami Avenue, 33130
+ 1 786 536 9194
ofyshop.com

10

Supply & Advise, Downtown
Classic menswear

After three years running a pop-up, New Yorker Jonathan Eyal decided to make things permanent for his multi-brand menswear shop in Downtown Miami. "I wasn't able to find a single dedicated store that sold a style that was practical, classic and interesting," he says.

Alden shoes line the wooden shelves and the clothing racks carry wardrobe staples from brands such as Gitman Vintage, Engineered Garments and tie specialist Drake's. Meanwhile, accessories including wallets and key rings by Floridian leather firm Makr can be found inside the glass display cases.
223 Southeast 1st Street, 33131
+ 1 305 960 2043
supplyandadvise.com

TOP PICKS:
01 Shoes by Alden
02 Wallet by Makr
03 Oxford shirts by Gitman Vintage

11

Apt 606, Design District
Sober staples

The edgy black-and-white aesthetic of this conceptual menswear boutique is a far cry from the occasionally over-cheery patterns of southern Floridian fashion.

Owners Lee Hylton and Dune Ivan favour minimalist aesthetics from highly respected brands. Discerning urbanites will find clothes by Raf Simons, Kris VanAssche, Christopher Kane, Alexander Wang, 3.1 Phillip Lim, Kenzo, Public School and Acne Studios, along with grooming products from the likes of Baxter of California and Cleanser 27.
89 Northeast 40th Street, 33137
+ 1 305 573 3330
apt606.com

Nope, I definitely didn't say that you haven't got a leg to stand on

Frankie, Sunset Harbour
Womenswear with dare

Run by long-time friends Cheryl Herger and Anna Deskins, this clothing shop stocks a youthful and often bold wardrobe. Clothing, accessories and bathing suits have a strong Antipodean bent, with Blesse'd Are the Meek and One Teaspoon helping shape the sultry collection. Herger's own line of clothing also hangs prominently in-store. Her collections are edited by Deskins, who is herself something of a retail veteran. The pair also have a second location on Sunset Drive in South Miami.
1891 Purdy Avenue, 33139
+ 1 786 479 4898
frankiemiami.com

Lost Boy Dry Goods, Downtown
Americana and more

Deer antlers hanging from the exposed brick walls, a smattering of family heirlooms and a vintage piano grab your attention when you step into this multi-brand men's and womenswear retailer.

Housed in the listed mid-century Alfred I DuPont Building, the high-ceilinged shop capitalises on customers' nostalgia for America's industrial age through its decor. "Unlike malls or department stores we aim to provide a unique shopping experience amid a historical and thought-provoking shop design," says co-founder Randy Alonso. He has picked out a range that sets classic denims and skincare products from brands such as New York's New Standard Edition and O'Douds from Houston alongside an insightful selection of vintage clothing, cowboy boots and vinyl.
157 East Flagler Street, 33131
+ 1 305 372 7303
lostboydrygoods.com

⑭
Sebastien James, Design District
Transatlantic tailoring

This European-inspired menswear
boutique also offers womenswear
through a partnership with Leslie
Benitah, ranging from sporty casual
pieces to cocktail dresses.
    Sebastien and Sandy Scemla's
shops in Miami and Paris have
been in business for more than 20
years. Their philosophy is to create
subtle European fashion – every
one of the double-stitched shirts
is handmade by seamstresses in
Barcelona – and adapt it to the all-
American male "seeking adventure
and seeking passion".
130 Northeast 40th Street,
Suite 2, 33137
+1 305 576 4470
sebastienjames.com

Spanish made
———
Having grown up visiting his
grandfather's clothing factory
in Paris, Sebastien James is
no stranger to manufacturing.
His label uses a series of
factories around Barcelona,
one of which dates back
to the 1930s: a boutique
workshop with a team of
22 seamstresses.

⑮
Sartorial Miami, Design District
Bespoke service

When it's time to kick off the
sandals and trade boardshorts for
a well-fitted suit, Sartorial Miami
is a good bet. Founded in late
2014 by sisters Tamara and Julia
Medvedeva, this shop in the Design
District stocks menswear from more
than 20 Italian brands, including
Kiton, Luigi Borelli and Svevo.
    There's also a shoe salon
showcasing trusted designers such
as Santoni and Sergio Rossi. Opt for
the full made-to-measure service and
customise every inch of your new
clothes, from the fabric, lining and
buttons to the stitching and finishing.
111 Northeast 40th Street, 33137
+1 305 707 6966
sartorialmiami.com

Concept stores
Miami lifestyle

① Wolfsonian shop, South Beach
Museum marvels

The shop's industrial interior pays homage to the museum's collection of postwar art-and-design objects, as portrayed in Wendy Kaplan's *Designing Modernity*. The book is but one of many items for sale here among design journals, exhibition catalogues, accessories such as watches and tableware, and a Wolfsonian Moleskine notebook.

Look out for exclusive merchandise by contemporary artists, including the "Thoughts on Democracy" poster series. For an afternoon pick-me-up, the café offers homemade nibbles.

1001 Washington Avenue, 33139
+ 1 305 535 2680
shop.wolfsonian.org

② En Avance, Design District
Moveable fashion feast

Karen Quinones opened her womenswear and concept home shop in 1993 in South Beach. Since then she has relocated from the super-mall surrounds of Lincoln Road and settled firmly in the Design District. En Avance's whitewashed interiors are home to collections from around the world, including offerings from Plein Sud and Katharine Hamnett, as well as homegrown talent such as Basile & Pape jewellery and award-winning Canadian womenswear brand Smythe.

"I have an understanding of the Miami woman," says Quinones, whose penchant for a minimal aesthetic doesn't jeopardise her attention to detail. The range of artsy homewares on offer adds up to a considered selection of modern collectibles.

53 Northeast 40th Street, 33137
+ 1 305 576 0056
enavance.com

TOP PICKS
01 Ceramic pieces by Fornasetti
02 Fragrances by Francis Kurkdjian
03 Embellished dresses by Gem
04 Beachwear by Magda Gomes
05 Silk-and-pashmina scarves by Florence Flameng

③
Malaquita, Wynwood
Mexico in Miami

Everything in design-and-clothing
shop Malaquita is made in Mexico.
An ode to the country's craft and
skills, simple modern jewellery by
Kult sits alongside clay ceramics
from Puebla. You can also find
colourful throws and skilfully made
clothing mixing contemporary
design with traditional techniques.

Opened in 2015, the shop is
the result of owners Ana Karen
Cervantes and Claudia Martinez's
efforts to preserve artisanal heritage
by collaborating with artists and
indigenous communities in Mexico.
2613 Northwest 2nd Avenue,
Unit 13, 33127
+1 786 615 4917
malaquitadesign.com

④
Frangipani, Wynwood
Eclectic avenue

Owner Jennifer Frehling has retail
design in her genes. Her parents
Robert and Nancy ran the well-
regarded Belvetro gallery in the
1990s and still operate the Oggetti
Designs store, which they opened
in 1975. Jennifer, deciding to follow
the family tradition, opened her
own Frangipani concept store in
2012 and has since added the shop
Flavorish Market to her growing
retail line-up.

A lively mix of sustainably made
knick-knacks adorn Frangipani's
stark-white geometric shelves. With
a strong home-team representation
including eclectic tableware and
colourful bags, the store seems
purpose-made to fill any gift-
shopping gaps.
2516 North West 2nd Avenue, 33127
+1 305 582 6396
frangipanimiami.com

TOP PICKS
01 Paper Town pop-up book
02 Bags and accessories by the
    Bluma Project
03 Leather coasters by Molly M
04 Beaded animal sculptures
    by Monkey Biz
05 Walnut bowls made in western
    Massachusetts using wood
    from fallen trees

Home and interior design
Inside knowledge

Specialist care
—
Each brand
has its own
interior
designer

Glo, El Portal
Lighting the way

This vintage dealer is a must-visit for fans of mid-century furniture and accessories. Founders and former flight attendants Rene Estevez and Tom Hutchinson honed their love of design while travelling the world.

Their growing collection recently prompted a move to a colossal new space in El Portal. Within it are pieces such as sideboards and chairs by designers Milo Baughman and Børge Mogensen, as well as an impressive range of lamps. International shipping is also available.
*555 Northeast 87th Street, 33138
+1 305 758 2727
glo.1stdibs.com*

4141 Design, Design District
World of interiors

Located opposite the Institute of Miami Art, this showroom boasts an impressive roll call of international design specialists that includes Swiss-based interiors company Vitra and Italian industrial specialists Zanotta.

This behemoth of luxury furniture and fittings is one of the largest on the continent; although it may seem daunting at first glance, specialists are always on hand to help decipher the seasonal ranges and assist with the finer details of shipping and installation.
*4141 North East 2nd Avenue,
Suite 115, 33137
+1 305 572 2900
4141design.com*

Show stopper

If the Floridian design scene has piqued your interest, book your trip to coincide with Design Miami in December. Unlike Salone or IMM Cologne, products at this annual event aren't always destined for production lines, allowing for a more playful and creative line-up.

Aubéry, North Miami
Mid-century mania

Born to French parents, Karine Aubéry has leaned on her international design nous to pull together this collection of furniture, lighting and art from the 1940s to the early 1980s. Opened in 2003, the shop is ever evolving and you'll find classics such as Noguchi coffee tables and chairs by Thonet.

Despite the big-name designers, Aubéry says she picks her pieces based on good materials and attractive silhouettes. "My gift is taking a classic piece and transforming it to fit current lifestyles," she says. "It's the French touch."
*1662 Northeast 123rd Street, 33181
+1 305 893 1015
Aubery.1stdibs.com*

On the wall
The shop also exhibits and sells original artwork

⑤
Pamm Shop, Downtown
Art of the sell

Located within the walls of Herzog & de Meuron's beautifully designed Pérez Art Museum Miami (Pamm) in Downtown's Museum Park, the Pamm Shop maintains the contemporary-museum aesthetic.

The shop sells a variety of gifts from artist-designed accessories to collectable books and, naturally, the requisite museum souvenirs. Pamm's are well above average however, and even if you're not in the market for a branded espresso cup you may be drawn to the weighty concrete desk set by Magnus Pettersen for Areaware or Orlando Fernandez Flores's jewellery. And when the brilliance on display in the museum gets too much, a pair of vintage-inspired sunglasses from Etnia Barcelona's International Klein Blue Collection may be in order.

1103 Biscayne Boulevard, 33132
+1 786 345 5694
pamm.org/shop

④
Holly Hunt, Design District
Home comforts

This award-winning two-storey showroom established in 2000 is fittingly located in the heart of the Design District, a destination for anyone with an eye for interiors and furniture. This light-flooded space showcases Texas-born Hunt's expansive collection, which launched in 1984 and has evolved into an international brand.

Whatever you're looking for in furnishings and interiors, from tables and textiles to lighting and floor coverings, the chances are Hunt has it covered.

3833 Northeast 2nd Avenue, 33137
+1 305 571 2012
hollyhunt.com

Shopping centre
One-stop browsing

①
Bal Harbour Shops, Miami Beach
Alfresco fashion

While an open-air Floridian shopping mall won't strike anyone as novel, Bal Harbour Shops stand out as a sophisticated retail oasis north of Miami Beach. Set in a former army barracks left over from the Second World War, the highly respected shopping destination has been family-owned by Whitman Family Development since it opened in 1965.

Over the years the place has expanded to offer some of the finest retail in Miami, including such high-end department stores as Nieman Marcus and Saks Fifth Avenue. The still-growing shopping centre also features powerhouse luxury brands such as Tomas Maier, Saint Laurent, Moncler, Miu Miu and Kiton, as well as speciality labels such as Torneau, La Perla and Wolford.

But the outdoor mall offers more than excellent shopping on its two floors. The open-air layout is filled with luscious tropical plants and kept cool with a well-designed fan system, so walking is as pleasant as taking a pew near one of its several koi ponds. And if you work up an appetite there are lots of tasty options to try; sushi restaurant Makoto does *otoro* worth writing home about.

9700 Collins Avenue, 33154
+1 305 866 0311
balharbourshops.com

I need air-con: my beard is perspiring somewhat

Specialist retail
Off-centre excellence

① Plant the Future, Wynwood
Beautiful blooms

Argentina-born Paloma Teppa and husband Yair Marcoschamer founded Plant the Future in 2008. Set in Wynwood's art district, it is both gallery and retail space for terrariums, desert gardens, orchid arrangements, airplant designs and a whimsical selection of jewellery.

Teppa's passion for flora means she only uses live plants, not cut flowers, for a sustainable alternative to traditional arrangements. Her sophisticated, inventive designs are best displayed at 1 Hotel in South Beach, where the pair have also opened a second shop.
2511 Northwest 2nd Avenue, 33127
+1 305 571 7177
plantthefuture.com

② Eberjey, South Beach
Get intimates

Eberjey is one of Miami's rare native brands and it couldn't be better suited to the sunshine state. Founded by Ali Mejia and Mariela Rovito in 1996, it offers US-made loungewear and swimwear collections that are perfect for relaxed South Beach afternoons.

The boutique is furnished in natural pastel shades that reflect the soft hues and delicate designs of its swimwear, lingerie and sleepwear collections, which are punctuated by stand-out pieces such as the bright-red So Solid Cora bikini.
1905 Purdy Avenue, 33139
+1 305 763 8839
eberjey.com

③ Wynwood Letterpress, Wynwood
Pencil in a visit

This design-and-stationery shop was started by Bridget Dadd and her husband in 2015 but its genesis goes way back. "I've been plotting it since I was a kid, hot-glueing my rubber collection to the inside of my dad's wooden cigar boxes," she says.

This is the perfect spot to find a unique gift – perhaps a set of pineapple-printed bamboo forks, some California-made Blackwing 602 pencils or quirky stationery from Rifle Paper Co. Keep an eye on its calendar for workshops in origami and bookbinding.
Suite 21, 2621 Northwest 2nd Avenue, 33127
+1 305 747 7559
wynwoodletterpress.com

⑤
I On The District, Design District
Quite a spectacle

More reminiscent of an art gallery than an optician, this eye-care and eyewear spot is a neighbourhood favourite. "We decided to give a lift to the optical industry and create a wardrobe for eyewear," says owner Irina Chovkovy, who opened shop in 2008.

The brands displayed within the crisp interiors are meticulously selected and carefully adhere to Chovkovy's strict criteria of quality materials and craftsmanship. Also available is a collection of vintage spectacles dating back to the 1930s, including frames made from wood, gold and buffalo horn. Private fittings and showings can be organised upon request and all frames can be customised with coloured and prescription lenses.
51 Northeast 40th Street, 33137
+1 305 573 9400
ionthedistrict.com

TOP PICKS
01 Eyewear by Jacques Marie Mage
02 Modern silhouettes by Andy Wolf
03 Sunglasses by Chrome Hearts
04 Iconic collections by Cutler and Gross
05 Lightweight frames by Ic! Berlin

④
Del Toro Shoes, Wynwood
Fusion footwear

Born in Italy and raised in Palm Beach, creative director Matthew Chevallard started Del Toro Shoes in 2005 with a collection of men's velvet slippers. It's since grown into an extensive range of men's and women's footwear that marries traditional Italian silhouettes with trainer culture. "We have our finger on the pulse of Miami," he says.

As the only Del Toro boutique, the shop offers a comprehensive range of the brand's brogues, slippers and trainers made from Nappa leather, suede and velvet.
2750 Northwest 3rd Avenue, Suite 22, 33127
+1 305 571 8253
deltoroshoes.com

Point and shoot
—
German photography legend Leica opened an outpost on Coral Gables' Miracle Mile in 2013. It stocks an extensive range of cameras and accessories, as well as binoculars and sport optics. With Miami as your backdrop, it's the ideal time to get snap-happy.

⑥
Genius Jones, Wynwood
Smalltime Einsteins

Bucking the trend of mass-produced baby goods, Daniel Kron founded children's shop Genius Jones in 2003. A beacon for quality design-oriented products for little ones, the Wynwood store is now in its second decade. "We've seen a whole generation of Miami's coolest kids grow up with products from here," says Kron.

Between the tipi tent and miniature art desks are clothing and furniture for newborns, toddlers and young children.
2800 Northeast 2nd Avenue, 33137
+1 305 571 2000
geniusjones.com

TOP PICKS
01 Colouring books by Keith Haring
02 Limited-edition Warhol-print prams by Bugaboo
03 Wooden blocks by Miller Goodman
04 Baby bag from Skip Hop
05 Highchair from Tripp Trapp

Swimwear

With the mercury rarely dipping below 20C, this seaside city is synonymous with swimwear. Here are our two favourites for beachwear shopping.

01 **Osklen, Miami Beach:**
Brazilian designer Oskar Metsavaht offers a range of high-end street wear and swimwear. The bold-silhouetted bikinis and bright men's trunks that recall Rio beach scenes are noted for their use of sustainably sourced materials.
osklen.com

02 **The Shop at The Standard, Miami Beach:**
From its collaborations with Kaws and José Parlá to lines from Frescobol Carioca and Made by Dawn, the shop stocks a range of men's and women's swimwear, sunglasses and hats. Sunscreen, towels and books complete its range of beach essentials.
standardhotels.com

All-in-one bathing suits will soon be a Miami staple, you watch

Tome will tell

The Bookstore in the Grove has earned a reputation as a creative melting pot in Coconut Grove since it was opened by Felice Dubin and Sandy Francis in 2007. The shop and organic café runs author nights and hosts a book club.
thebookstoreinthegrove.com

7
Books & Books, Coral Gables
Laidback and literate

This bibliophile paradise was founded when Mitchell Kaplan's enthusiasm for literature drove him to drop out of law school to open a shop. "This is my way of helping to further the dialogue surrounding literary culture," he says.

There's a reading room for children and an international newsstand, while customers can have books signed at author events held amid the collection of art, architecture and design titles. Enjoy a happy-hour drink or a proper lunch at the in-store café run by award-winning chef Allen Susser.
265 Aragon Avenue, 33134
+1 305 442 4408
booksandbooks.com

⑧
Sweat Records, Little Haiti
Vinyl venue

Boasting Miami's best selection of
LPs, CDs and cassettes, this is the
place to pick up your latest record, a
cup of Panther coffee and maybe
a tote bag too.

Situated next door to the
musical institution Churchill's Pub
(the shop's home for two years after
a hurricane destroyed its original
location), Lauren Reskin's shop is a
music store that doubles as a vegan
café and event space. The mural
by artist CPI features the musical
heroes you'll hear being played
inside, from Iggy Pop to Thurston
Moore.
5505 Northeast 2nd Avenue, 33137
+ 1 786 693 9309
sweatrecordsmiami.com

Hotel retail
Pick of the lobby shops

①
Making an entrance
Check in, check-out

From Latin American holidaymakers
and European creatives to domestic
weekend explorers, Miami is always
playing host. So it's little wonder
that retail culture has reconfigured
the hotel-lobby gift shop.

Nestled in the ornate reception
of The Miami Beach Edition (*see
page 22*) is ❶ *Limited Edition*. Steven
Giles from luxury lifestyle store Base
(*see page 50*) oversees a collection
that includes men's bags by Phillip
Lim, grooming products by Ernest
Supplies and a worldly selection of
books, magazines and collectables.

With 20 years of hotel experience
between them, Greg Melvin and
Paolo Ambu partnered with the
Collins Avenue hotel to open their
shop ❷ *Babalú* at the Raleigh Miami
Beach Boutique in 2010. "There's
a thread of symphony between the
product mix and the architecturally
significant hotel," says Melvin, whose
range of beachwear and collectables
is influenced by the prominent
hotel's art deco interiors.

For jewellery from Ela Stone,
Pascale Monvoisin and Miami-based
Hües, drop into Parisian-inspired
❸ *Violet & Grace* in South Beach's
1 Hotel (*see page 21*). The shop is
run by German former model Ina
Lettmann and her business partner,
Croatian film producer Rita Rusic.

Where to find them

01 Limited Edition
    2901 Collins Avenue,
    33140
    +1 786 257 4500
    editionhotels.com
02 Babalú
    1775 Collins Avenue,
    33139
    +1 305 612 1160
    ilovebabalu.com
03 Violet & Grace
    1901 Collins Avenue,
    33139
    +1 305 534 1500
    violetandgrace.com

Things we'd buy
—— Objects of desire

Miami's perpetual warm weather doesn't just draw a holiday crowd: it also attracts some of the finest brands. While there are plenty of global retailers to browse in Bal Harbour and the Design District, you'll also find a growing stable of independent boutiques such as The Webster and Base.

Creative Miamians are fashioning everything from nautical-themed jewellery and loafers to savoury jams. So if you're keen to arrive home with more than just a little sand in your suitcase, peruse the products on our list and pick up the perfect souvenir.

01 Makr backpack from Supply & Advise *supplyandadvise.com*
02 Shoes by Del Toro *deltoroshoes.com*
03 Miami Beach Suncare from Boucher Brothers *boucherbrothers.com*
04 Ceramics by Malaquita Design *malaquitadesign.com*
05 Custom candle by The Webster *thewebstermiami.com*
06 *Forager: A Subjective Guide to Miami's Edible Plants* from Books & Books *booksandbooks.com*
07 Cigar by Cuba Tobacco Cigar Co *cubatobaccocigarco.com*
08 Jammy Yummy vegetable jams from Miam Café *miamcafe.com*
09 Laurie's Pantry granola from Flavorish Market *flavorishmarket.com*
10 Stiltsville pilsner by Concrete Beach Brewery *concretebeachbrewery.com*
11 Honey from Mandolin Aegean Bistro *mandolinmiami.com*
12 Tote from Mimo Market *mimomarket.com*
13 Arnold Steiner pocket squares from Mimo Market *mimomarket.com*
14 Makr copper tumblers from Supply & Advise *supplyandadvise.com*
15 Coffee mugs by Pamm *pamm.org*
16 Swimming cap by Warby Parker *warbyparker.com*
17 Sunglasses by Warby Parker *warbyparker.com*
18 Frescobol Carioca bat and ball from Babalú *ilovebabalu.com*
19 Swimwear by Eberjey *eberjey.com*
20 Juices by Jucy Lu *jucylu.com*
21 Keyrings by Warby Parker *warbyparker.com*
22 Cuban-style coffee from La Carreta *lacarreta.com*
23 Ron de Jeremy Reserva rum from Total Wine *totalwine.com*
24 Frescobol Carioca Panama hat from Babalú *ilovebabalu.com*

01 Fragrance and candles by
Base *baseworld.com*
02 Miansai watch from Base
baseworld.com
03 Stationery and keyrings
by Wynwood Letterpress
wynwoodletterpress.com
04 Miansai jewellery from Base
baseworld.com

05 *Four Florida Moderns* from
Books & Books
booksandbooks.com
06 *Mi Tierra* vinyl album by Gloria
Estefan from Sweat Records
sweatrecordsmiami.com
07 Textiles by Malaquita Design
malaquitadesign.com

12 essays
—— Making sense of Miami

1
Gaudy gratification
Art Basel
by Robert Bound,
Monocle Culture editor

2
Buenos días, América
Latin Miami
by Ed Stocker, Monocle
New York bureau chief

3
Take two
Miami at the movies
by Diliana Alexander,
production studio director

4
Painting a picture
Creative city
by Craig Robins,
property developer

5
Illuminating experience
Neon signs
by Marie-Sophie Schwarzer,
Monocle writer and
researcher

6
Staying afloat
Stiltsville
by Antoinette Baldwin,
construction manager

7
Stream of consciousness
Miami's literature
by P Scott Cunningham,
poet and translator

8
In with the old
Historical Miami
by Megan Cross Schmitt,
preservation officer

9
Money talks
Property development
by Paul S George,
professor of history

10
Miami nice
Improved reputation
by Liv Lewitschnik,
Monocle contributing editor

11
Casting a spell
Miami's magic
by Rob Goyanes,
poet and critic

12
Court of appeal
Jai alai
by Jason Li,
Monocle Toronto
deputy bureau chief

Try my drinking game: swig every time you read 'Miami'

ESSAY 01

Gaudy gratification
Art Basel

———

Absurdly garish, incredibly international and packed with personalities, Art Basel Miami Beach is as colourful and entertaining as the art it's showing. But no need to be snobby about it: it's about the most fun you can have in town.

by Robert Bound, Monocle

If you're not paying your own hotel bill, the best week to visit Miami is the first one in December when Art Basel Miami Beach rolls into town. As you explore the boulevard-wide aisles of art at the Miami Beach Convention Center (was it built for selling aeroplanes or supertankers?) you'll believe this is the best place in the world in which to see and sell art. Maybe later you'll wonder if it's just a pretty ordinary place to see and sell art but that it happens to be in the world's sunniest, silliest city.

Later still (after a rum) you might wonder if what you really like is that this week's festivities are the fun, slutty sister of the stern, matronly, seriously Swiss original Art Basel and the high-class but unsmiling hooker that is Art Basel Hong Kong. Then, in the morning, you'll be glad you didn't commit such a crass analogy to paper.

While you're wondering these things you'll see, through your Ray-Bans, blue-chip galleries run by linen-suited art dealers in fluro trainers. They'll be selling big, bright canvases and easy-to-like photography to deep-tanned art collectors too rich to care about putting on a jacket or what people think of their his'n'hers, cake-in-the-rain plastic surgery.

Important works by Andy Warhol, Jasper Johns and Jean-Michel Basquiat seem to wash up on the shoreline as if a supertanker (what did I tell you?) skippered by mega-gallerist Larry Gagosian has run aground and shed its practically priceless load. Along with the jellyfish that end up on Miami Beach every morning there are million-dollar flotsam and art-historically important jetsam all over the shop.
I *love* it.

Miami's great strength is that it doesn't confuse good art with good taste, of which

"You'll see blue-chip galleries run by linen-suited art dealers in fluro trainers"

**Miami drinking
spots**
—
**01 The Martini Bar
at The Raleigh**
Starched, proper, old-school.
**02 Basement bowling alley at
The Miami Beach Edition**
White Russians and strikes.
03 Mac's Club Deuce
Quite simply the definitive dive.

it has little. Praise be! Good taste is the bane of good art, which is all about bigger, better and deeper things than looking clever, tucking your shirt in and behaving well enough to be invited back next time. Miami doesn't give a fig for all that, which is why you stand a good chance of bumping into a real-life, paint-flecked artist in this bright-eyed and bushy-tailed town. Artists often feign disdain for the circus of the art fairs but in sunny Miami a couple of weeks shy of Christmas you'll see some creative types used to wearing inscrutable smiles or subtle frowns laughing their head off or dancing to Beyoncé (the real one). Miami is a great place to be an artist because it behaves like one: it doesn't care what you or anyone else thinks.

In Miami, where there is great wealth but also a hell of a lot of seaside, taste is funny. You might be invited into the house of an eminent octogenarian art collector for a party at which, behind Roman pillars and cherubic finials, big-name hip-hop stars are performing in the garden in a fog

of happy smoke. Or perhaps an abode where bow-tied barmen are making their life easier by handing out bottles of rum and glasses of ice and lime, and you've just been asked by a couple you know from somewhere "to come upstairs and help them take some pictures". And the place is full of – *strewn* with – famous and priceless things. (Oh, they didn't mean take some pictures: they meant take some pictures *of them*.)

Think I'm over-egging the pudding? To refresh your memory, we're talking about Miami in the first week of December when many amusing art-world people living in Europe or New York will have either been bored to tears by heavy drizzle, grey skies and umbrella fatigue or will have simply been frozen stiff for two months. Art dealers from Latin America will be happily cooling off "up north" and Argentinians will be indulging their deep-seated Euro fantasy by tying sweaters around their shoulders as if for a promenade around Lake Como. The odd European gallery director will tell you that Miami is, in fact, bang in the middle of their far-too-busy, thoroughly international year of fair- and biennale-hopping, and that frankly it's all a bit much. But for most this is their grand end-of-term party and a sight to behold (and be held by). Every December for more than a decade a new hotel – a study in white walls, deceptively hard-wearing linens

and built-in loucheness – opens its door and dancefloor in time for Art Basel. It's the week when the city hitches up its skirts – just when you thought it already had.

Sometimes the art crowd gets all Prince of Denmark and has recently – but wherefore it knows not – lost all its mirth. If anyone should forget what a "goodly frame" is, it shouldn't be the art world. But you know what? Come December, all those curatorially minded, jetlag-diminished cats need a bit of beach and a bit of quality time in a town that wears everything, including its learning, feather-lightly. Don't roll your eyes at the show of it all and pretend you wish you were in the harrowing cold in a converted hangar in Dresden looking at post-industrial sculptures. Quite a lot of art is noticeably improved by being viewed through a heat haze. Give in to the beach. — (M)

ABOUT THE WRITER: Robert Bound is MONOCLE's Culture editor. He also hosts the *Culture Show* on our radio station Monocle 24; tune in every Monday at 19.00 GMT and 14.00 EST (or download the podcast). Look out for his colourful trousers and sharp jackets while he elbows his way past the clip-board crew at Miami's best parties during Art Basel.

ESSAY 02
Buenos días, América
Latin Miami

⸺

An American version of a Latin American city is how many fondly describe this sun-kissed Floridian metropolis. And with large, powerful and vocal Latino communities, it's not hard to see why.

*by Ed Stocker,
Monocle*

"This isn't the US, this is Latin America." My Colombian taxi driver is cruising around the spaghetti junctions of Miami under a relentlessly battering Florida sun – and he has a point. Miami may have infinitesimal guises that cater to the broad church that heads here – from the perma-tanned muscle boys to the pasty "northerners" in town for a dousing of culture – but one thing most visitors agree on is that Miami doesn't feel like anywhere else in the US.

Walk around and you're often more likely to hear Spanish than English. It may have the rapid pace and swallowed "s" sounds of a Caribbean drawl or the dramatic, almost Italian inflections of Argentinian *castellano* but it announces one fact loud and clear: the Latin population has made Miami its home. And this isn't an impoverished community working menial jobs. Heaven forbid. The bright lights and palm trees are aspirational for many upwardly mobile Latin Americans who are looking for a place to shop till they drop or park cash away from unstable economies back home.

For decades, leftist presidents in the Spanish-speaking Americas, such as Hugo Chávez and Evo Morales, have tried to create this concept of pan-American unity. It's had a modicum of success but never has that dream been realised quite so completely – and so entirely by accident – than in Miami. Here Latinos from El Salvador to Ecuador bow together before the altar of sun, sea and social security.

Not that many of the Latinos who have made Miami their home are exactly budding revolutionaries. Florida's southern tip is just 144km away from Cuba and many of Miami's million-plus former islanders are staunchly anti-Castro. Indeed, the city hosts one of the regime's most critical voices, Radio and TV Martí, beamed directly (when it can get through the signal blockers) to the island. Whenever Cuba is in the headlines, journalists flock to the community's cafés to get interviews from expats, well aware of the reaction they'll get. If they're lazy they'll probably head to the renowned Café Versailles, a Cuban pit-stop so successful that it even has an outpost at Miami International Airport.

Versailles branching out into the airport shows how popular – and mass-market – Brand Cuba has become in Miami. There may be plenty of gringos who don't speak the lingo but they still interact with the Latin community. And the reason why probably boils down to one daily ritual: coffee. Cubans do the best brew in town and *un cafecito* – a small coffee packed with teeth-decaying amounts of sugar – gives you the sort of caffeine punch perfect for a day in the tropics.

"The Latin community, so established and yet so attached to its customs, offers a fascinating insight into multiracial, multilingual Miami"

Cuban coffee lingo

01 Cafecito
Classic fare: a single shot with lots of sugar.
02 Cortadito
Espresso topped off with a small amount of steamed milk.
03 Colada
Several espresso shots in a big cup, designed for sharing.

One of my favourite places in Miami is El Palacio de los Jugos on West Flagler Street. It's a humble food spot, just off a main road in an unremarkable part of town. None of the surrounding shops have signs in English: everything is *en español*. El Palacio serves simple juices and vast portions of Cuban food (meat, rice, plantain et al). It's great for people-watching as rickety ceiling fans – half of them broken – whir noisily above an open eating area, occasionally spraying water in a bid to counter the heat. Here you'll spot families and lovers; medallions, tattoos and big earrings; a man desperately trying to sell bootleg perfume; and a stray cat looking on with boredom.

Miami is, of course, a diverse place. And not just because of Latinos from Venezuela, Honduras, Cuba and everywhere else in between. But it's that very Latin community, so established and yet so attached to its customs, that offers a fascinating insight into multiracial, multilingual Miami in all its glory. And as relations with Cuba thaw further over the coming years – and the population continues to swell – the Miami crucible will make for fascinating watching. Yes indeed: this really is a Latin city. — (M)

ABOUT THE WRITER: Ed Stocker has been MONOCLE's New York bureau chief since 2014. Before making the move he was based in Argentina for four years, where he was our Buenos Aires correspondent. The accents and architecture (not to mention the tropical juices) are what draw him to Miami.

Take two
Miami at the movies

Having fallen behind in the box-office queue, the city is taking centre stage once again with a plethora of independent film-makers, cinemas, regular movie events and festivals.

by Diliana Alexander, production studio director

Remember philosopher Søren Kierkegaard's quote, "The more a person limits himself, the more resourceful he becomes"? Independent film-makers like me have that quote tattooed on our hearts. And as technological advances make good and affordable equipment becomes available to more of us, we are finally being given the opportunity to work outside the system and tell unique stories. And unique stories are what Miami has in abundance.

When I first moved to The Magic City in 2009, my expectation of it – a place I had never visited before – involved a combination of palm trees, mildly distressed flamingos, fast boats, good-looking girls, criminals and, beneath it all, a driving 1980s synth. I wasn't entirely off the mark but this was just one side of it. This clichéd image of Miami (and with it, our collective memory of Sonny Crockett, Rico Tubbs and Tony Montana) is fading like the glamour of the Versace mansion. Today it is a city that has

reinvented itself through thriving design and art scenes, which have improved the city's reputation and attracted creative talent from all over the world. Another major aspect of this reinvention – one that is sometimes overlooked – is its film industry.

In the late 1990s, Miami was the third-biggest film production centre in the US after Los Angeles and New York. The combination of an eternal summer and tax incentives attracted Hollywood productions, commercials, fashion shoots and music videos. But then things changed. As surrounding US states introduced competitive tax incentives, Florida's conservative government took the opposite route, refusing to extend them beyond a certain cap. As film incentives dried up, big-budget productions dwindled, though the Spanish TV market continued to flourish.

Yet with the speed of technological change over the past decade, film-making has become more affordable, accessible and ultimately more diverse, leading to an influx of independent film-makers, many of whom are now choosing to stay put in their city. The most prolific and successful Miami-based production company is Rakontur, which made *Cocaine Cowboys* – a documentary looking at the drug wars of the 1970s and 1980s – and *The U*, a feature about the championship history of the University of Miami Hurricanes football team. The film-makers at Corner of the Cave, now a popular production

Miami festivals

01 Miami International Film Festival, March
miamifilmfestival.com
02 III Points Festival, October
iiipoints.com
03 Miami Book Fair International, November
miamibookfair.com

"This clichéd image of Miami is fading like the glamour of the Versace Mansion. The city has reinvented itself through its thriving art scenes"

company, had their break via a successful online campaign that financed their first film, the festival darling *Far Out Isn't Far Enough.* And then there's indie hero film-maker Kenny Riches telling Miami magical realism stories; his most recent work, *The Strongest Man,* premiered at the Sundance Film Festival in 2015. And with more quality films in the pipeline you can expect to continue seeing Miami stories on the big screen.

With independent film-makers and production companies now well established, art-house cinemas and festivals have followed suit. The most successful venue is probably the edgy O Cinema with three locations across the city. My favourite is O Cinema 1.0 in Wynwood, which is one of the city's main art districts. It includes a gallery showcasing Miami's visual artists from the ArtCenter South Florida, an independent shop, a film library and a cosy courtyard with monthly alfresco screenings.

The most popular night over here is *OMG! Dinner & a Movie,* where you can sample different food while feasting your eyes and feeding your soul. This is also the best place to meet home-grown film talent. Although I admit that I might be biased, since O Cinema Wynwood is also the home of FilmGate, the non-profit organisation I head. In the past three years it has been inviting Florida-based film-makers from Key West to West Palm to screen their short-format projects here, at a night we call, with tongues in cheeks, *I'm Not Gonna Move to LA.*

Elsewhere, the classy Miami Beach Cinematheque had a humble beginning in a store on Española Way but has since moved to the historic city hall. It has a velvety atmosphere and thoughtful programming, highlighting festival winners and director retrospectives. Its *Speaking in Cinema* series is a bi-monthly event hosting one director and two film critics – one from Miami, one international – to discuss the director's motivation, philosophy and technique. In a nutshell, it's cinematic geek bliss where you can meet visual storytellers in an intimate atmosphere. Meanwhile, over in Little Havana The Tower Theater specialises in Ibero-American cinema. It's run by the Miami International Film Festival and its programme director Orlando Rojas is an iconic Cuban film-maker with impeccable taste.

Speaking of film fests, whether it's the star-studded Miami International Film Festival, the stylish Gay and Lesbian Film Festival or their smaller sibling Key West Film Festival, Miami seems to cater to all tastes. In addition, each February our organisation hosts the creative conference FilmGate Interactive, which attracts more than 5,000 film professionals who are looking to explore how the newest developments in technology – from virtual-reality glasses to 8K resolution – are influencing the future of film-making and entertainment.

We do hope big-budget films return to Miami but until they do, independent film-makers will remain, taking risks, managing constraints, documenting and distilling the magic of the city. Let Miami continue to reclaim its rightful place as a film-making centre, an other-worldly city – wild, tropical and irreverent – where anything can happen. — (M)

ABOUT THE WRITER: Diliana Alexander moved to Miami in 2009. She is the executive director of FilmGate Interactive, a Miami-based non-profit production studio that originates and screens immersive media projects. Her favourite film made in Miami is Spike Jonze's *Adaptation.*

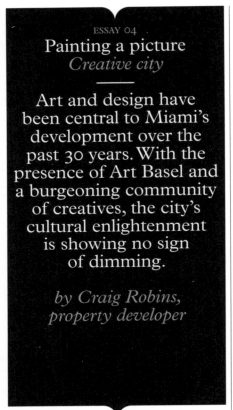

ESSAY 04

Painting a picture
Creative city

Art and design have been central to Miami's development over the past 30 years. With the presence of Art Basel and a burgeoning community of creatives, the city's cultural enlightenment is showing no sign of dimming.

*by Craig Robins,
property developer*

I became very interested in art during a year spent studying in Barcelona. When I returned to Miami in 1984 and attended law school I began to invite artists to come to the city and paint. I had no clue about what I wanted to do: I didn't think I was going to go into law; going into property, my father's business, was appealing on a practical level but it wasn't inspiring; and becoming an art dealer didn't seem sensible in Miami.

Looking for studios for the artists I was working with, I turned to South Beach – and the Art Deco District – where I had grown up. At the time, the early 1980s, the area had a dwindling elderly population and these magnificent buildings were home to a retirement community. I realised that there was something really special here so I teamed up with developer Tony Goldman and we formed a partnership to buy a couple of properties. My first tenant was the artist Keith Haring. At the time he was painting these stores in New York called "Pop Shop" and I got him to do a variant in Miami that was called "Wham Bam".

Things took off from there. People started painting the buildings in pastel colours thanks to this idea from a visionary named Leonard Horowitz. The façades looked great and became an amazing backdrop for photography.

World-class creative people were discovering South Beach – but there were no hotels. Chris Blackwell (the founder of Island Records) and I became partners and we bought the Marlin Hotel. We built 12 hotel rooms; we also

> **Three key pieces from Robins' collection**
> ———
> 01 Richard Tuttle, 'Untitled', 1967
> 02 Marcel Duchamp, '3 Standard Stoppages', 1913 (replica, 1964)
> 03 John Baldessari, 'Clement Greenberg', 1966-1968

had a Jamaican restaurant and a recording studio. I always thought that South Beach was as much a movement as a place. I saw it as a rebirth of Miami but a new version.

People recognised the success of Miami Beach by the mid-1990s but they didn't think it could cross the bridge onto the mainland. There was virtually nothing there at the time. So I got this idea that the movement – the spirit of South Beach – could work in the Miami Design District, probably the most central location in the whole of the city.

"I love that this design show was born in Miami. It wasn't born in New York or London or Paris; it's from here. It's a big deal"

It had been a centre for furniture design but like South Beach it had become rundown because of the success of a nearby shopping mall. And so I began to buy buildings there and after accumulating a significant portfolio – today my partners and I own about 70 per cent of the property in the district – the first thing we did was bring back what had historically been there: furniture design.

I decided that I was going to bring back design and put it on the streets. There would be actual shopfronts instead of having the furniture hidden in malls. Salone del Mobile in Milan was where I first saw the entire community of

the city – plus advocates of design from all over the world – get together and celebrate it.

And so a few years later, in the late 1990s, when I met Art Basel's Sam Keller and he suggested we bring the event to Miami, a light started flashing in my head. I thought that if we could bring the best art fair in the world to this sexy, hedonistic, fun city, combining that entertainment component of Miami with the solidity and tradition of Art Basel – while creating almost an art version of Salone with its citywide events – this could be a huge thing.

Then in 2005 I was approached about putting on a design show during Art Basel, which would become Design Miami. It was the first fair devoted to collectible design that was exuberant and lively and it has become the premiere global forum for the design community with a second annual show in Basel. I love that it was born in Miami. It wasn't born in New York or London or Paris; it's from here. For me that was a big deal because it showed the potential of our young but emerging city. Miami is definitely a city of the future. — (M)

ABOUT THE WRITER: Craig Robins founded Dacra in 1987, a property company that regenerates districts in Miami by combining architecture, art, design and cultural programmes. Robins was integral in the redevelopment of the Art Deco District in South Beach in the 1980s and is also an avid art collector and a principal of Art Basel Miami Beach.

ESSAY 05
Illuminating experience
Neon signs

When it comes to bright lights, Miami's neon is as iconic as Las Vegas's Strip or New York's Times Square. We chart the flickering existence of the city's nostalgic beacons.

by Marie-Sophie Schwarzer, Monocle

In New York, skyscrapers act as signposts; in Miami it's the city's neon lights. Dazzling displays deck the art deco hotels along Ocean Drive and the Mimo (Miami modernist architecture) hotels on Biscayne Boulevard. At dusk they ignite one by one, casting a surreal florescent midnight sun over the city and its suburbs.

Indeed, it's impossible to overlook the 1935-established Colony Hotel with its dizzying electric-blue signage vying for your attention where Ocean Drive meets 7th Street; nor the shimmering curvy red signature above the Clevelander Hotel a few blocks north. Miami doesn't need streetlights or moonlight for that matter: its streets shimmer with nocturnal colour. It may not have the wattage of Las Vegas or Tokyo but Miami's neon lights are tied to the identity of this young city – a metropolis that reached adolescence in the age of neon.

In 1898, just two years after the founding of Miami, British chemists

Sir William Ramsay and Morris Travers unearthed the gaseous element that would lend Miami its characteristic glow. They called it neon, from the Greek *neos* ("new"). In its natural state it is quite unremarkable. As a member of the noble-gases family – comprising argon, radon, krypton, xenon and helium – it is colourless, odourless, tasteless and non-flammable. Yet apply electric voltage to electrodes at the ends of a glass tube containing the gas and it begins to radiate a burning red light.

It was the French engineer Georges Claude who made this pioneering discovery in 1902 and unveiled the first commercial neon sign at a Parisian barbershop almost a decade later. "Palais Coiffeur" read the luminous light, luring patrons inside like moths to a flame. Yet it wasn't Europe but the US that fomented a neon revolution. It landed on the shores of the New World in 1923 when Claude installed the first US sign at the Los Angeles Packard Car dealership. Soon his "liquid fire" spread across the states, from California to New York and Florida. It became the de facto symbol of the modern age.

By the 1920s, America was living it up in true Great Gatsby style and the introduction of Henry Ford's Model T car sparked the country's love affair with the automobile. During this period, Miami's population skyrocketed from about 5,000 in 1910 to 30,000 within a decade, which gave rise to the nickname "The Magic

---

Neon signs to savour

01 11th Street Diner, South Beach
Art deco gem.
02 Ball & Chain
Little Havana's neon pride.
03 The Colony Hotel, South Beach
Landmark on Ocean Drive.

City". Thousands of sunseekers took full advantage of their new-found freedom and drove thousands of miles to reach the southern state, encouraged by advertising gimmicks headlined by Carl Fisher – the builder and so-called father of Miami Beach – who put up a giant lit billboard in New York's Times Square broadcasting "It's June in Miami".

"Apart from accenting the geometric façades, neon arrows and signs became requisites for the cornucopia of hotels, diners and bars"

It had the desired effect and Miami soon found itself in the midst of a building boom. Sleek American streamline moderne-style buildings shot up left and right, taking art deco to the next level and infusing it with a dynamic touch that reflected the country's technological progress and defined neon as an integral part of 20th-century architecture. Apart from accenting the geometric façades, neon arrows and signs became requisites for the cornucopia of hotels, diners and bars scrambling for patrons.

The carefree years were short-lived though; in 1926 the Great Miami Hurricane extinguished the lights, if only for a while. After the Second World War the city recovered much of its lost splendour and once again automobile-borne holidayers arrived in droves. Miami catered to America's car culture with wide roads and rows of motels, especially along the city's north-south artery, Biscayne Boulevard. By the mid-20th century the boulevard was a jungle of neon placards advertising air-conditioning and vacancies in bright blues and reds, figuratively waving at drivers speeding past. The Shalimar Motel, opened in 1951, called attention to itself with its delta-wing pylon neon sign; so too the Seven Seas Motel with its vivid lettering and the South Pacific Motel with its large-scale fluorescent display. But the star of the bunch was and still is the 1953 Vagabond Motel designed by architect Robert Swartburg, which stands opposite the legendary Coppertone Girl, a house-sized neon sign made by Tropicalites in 1958. What was all the rage in the 1950s slowly faded out of fashion a decade later and as Biscayne Boulevard's characteristic motels fell into disrepair, the red radiance dissipated too and neon moved from the streets to the artist's studio.

Perhaps it was *Miami Vice*, perhaps the cycle of time or maybe just the city's nostalgic nature but before long neon returned. Today, more than half a century later, Biscayne Boulevard resembles its old self once more. The dilapidated Vagabond has been given a new lease of life by developer Avra Jain and for $65,000, NeonSigns Solutions reproduced the motel's iconic signs and brought the familiar flicker back to the historic Mimo neighbourhood.

"I think we associate neon with colourful, happy times. Memories of when we were younger, taking road trips as part of our family vacation," says Jain. "Whether it's Vegas or the roadside motels and diners, more than the playful eye candy, it's those memories that make it all the more special." — (M)

ABOUT THE WRITER: German-born Marie-Sophie Schwarzer is a writer and researcher for MONOCLE. Before relocating to London, she lived in the US and studied journalism at Columbia University in New York. Her favourite thing about Miami? The endless beaches and galleries (besides the neon signs, obviously).

ESSAY 06
Staying afloat
Stiltsville

It's been buffeted by strong winds and political forces but Miami's most inspiring neighbourhood is still standing – on stilts in the middle of Biscayne Bay.

by Antoinette Baldwin, construction manager

Away from the condo canyons, the art scene, the shops and the Cuban coffee, there's an idyllic place with a colourful history, 10km from Downtown and a mile south of Cape Florida lighthouse at the tip of Key Biscayne. Its name? Stiltsville.

"No one who chances upon the phenomenon of Stiltsville for the first time will ever forget the sight of homes that hover above the waters like structure from a dream," writes author and historian Les Standiford. Only accessible by boat, these structures are built on the shallow sand and tidal flats that separate Biscayne Bay from the Atlantic Ocean. There are navigable channels that cut through the flats and one of these, Biscayne Channel, is Stiltsville's main "street". The houses lined up along it give it the appearance of a city block.

My husband Gail and I understand the power Stiltsville has over the imagination. He first learnt about the place when he was hired as an architect in the early 1970s to prepare plans for "a house on the water". Little did he know that the house was actually in the middle of the bay and that in two years he would end up buying it with four partners.

When architecture firm Herzog & de Meuron was asked what inspired its design for the new waterfront Pérez Art Museum Miami in Museum Park, the response was that it was the houses of Stiltsville, seen during a boat tour of Biscayne Bay. Yet the story of the place is as old as Miami itself, taking you back to another time when the city was known as Miamah and the houses were known as The Shacks.

They had a use back then when shipwrecking and channel-

The best of Biscayne Bay

---

01 **Cape Florida Lighthouse**
A room with a view.
02 **Paul George's Stiltsville & Biscayne Bay tour**
Catch the Miami historian's lowdown.
03 **Visit a Stiltsville house**
Get out there and see it for yourself.

"No one who chances upon Stiltsville for the first time will ever forget the sight of homes that hover above the waters"

dredging were the main jobs in the area and Biscayne Channel was the only deep-water access to Biscayne Bay (until the Government Cut inlet in 1905 contributed to the creation of Miami Beach).

As Miami grew, Stiltsville morphed into a place for weekend getaways. Historians have found records that there were 12 shacks in 1922; by the 1940s, the most famous shack belonged to fisherman and retired lighthouse keeper "Crawfish" Eddie Walker. He sold bait and beer from his floating home and was known for his crayfish "chilau" chowder.

The place that really put The Shacks on the map was the Quarterdeck Club, built in 1940 by Commodore Edward Turner. It opened with great fanfare and soon became the most popular spot in Miami. But by 1950 a hurricane caused enough damage that it never regained its popularity and it was eventually destroyed by fire in 1961.

Hurricanes have defined the beginning and end of most of the houses and 1992 was an unforgettable year. Hurricane Andrew bulldozed the area with its Category 5 fury and five-metre storm surges that left Stiltsville with only seven houses standing. Some houses disappeared entirely from the bay. But by then Biscayne National Park had expanded its northern boundary just enough to include Stiltsville and that meant that no new houses were allowed to be constructed. Then in 1999, when the old bay-bottom leases with the State of Florida had expired, Stiltsville became the property of the federal government that wanted the houses to be removed. And so the campaign to save old Stiltsville began.

In all, 130,000 signatures were collected and hundreds of letters of support sent from senators, mayors, celebrities, historical associations and artists. Environmentalists wanted the owners out and the houses preserved as nurseries for sea life. There was an appearance in Federal Court and a bill introduced in Congress. Finally, President Clinton signed an appropriation bill that included an extension of the leases. This allowed enough time for the National Park Service to enter into an agreement with the former owners, effectively saving Stiltsville. The ex-owners are now caretakers and members of Stiltsville Trust, whose mission is to preserve the colourful shacks and provide public use.

Stiltsville has been the setting for many of life's celebrations;

even senator Ted Kennedy chose it as the location to celebrate his engagement party to his second wife in 1991. It's a place where people catch their first bonefish, learn to swim, watch their first sunrise or even choose to spend eternity by having their ashes scattered here.

That heaven-on-Earth sentiment was shared by Florida governor LeRoy Collins. A frequent visitor to The Shacks, in 1959 he gave a scrapbook to his host Jimmy Ellenburg, the unofficial mayor of Stiltsville, whose last house is still standing here. On one of its pages he wrote, "Jimmy Ellenburg, when the time comes when I say so long to this life I hope the great beyond seems a lot like your cabin in the sea." — (M)

ESSAY 07

Stream of consciousness
Miami's literature

—

For its writers – the ones who stayed and the ones who moved away – this vibrant, chaotic city inspires and infuriates in equal measure. That said, its lack of a defined, glitzy literary scene is one of its greatest assets.

by P Scott Cunningham, poet and translator

Miami is not a literary city like New York or Chicago. It's more like Paris. Not Paris right now but Paris 170 years ago. The Paris of Balzac and Zola: a sprawling metropolis struggling to keep up with its own rate of change. "Miamians themselves have been so busy making history they do not often stop to consider how it happened." The author Helen Muir said that in 1953 but it's still true today.

Balzac would be delighted by Miami's fragmented cacophony and the possibilities that chaos presents for literature. The city is so teeming with culture that it's strange we're always being accused of not having any. Perhaps what the critics mean is that our culture is not the one that flatters their own tastes? Miami's constant growth and diversity does make it a little bit *arroz con mango* (rice with mango: a local term for things that don't go together) but after a while the discord starts to look like a style. Salvadoran *pupusa* joints face Cuban

ABOUT THE WRITER: Antoinette Baldwin is founder of Stiltsville's artist-in-residence programme. She lives in Coconut Grove, works as a construction manager and along with her husband Gail, an architect, is a caretaker of Stiltsville House 1, the Baldwin Sessions House.

shrimp shacks. Bike paths wind past sleeping alligators and for many years the best Spanish-language bookshop was in the car park of DIY shop Home Depot.

Because Miami is constantly in flux it can be cruel and unsympathetic, especially to writers. The great novelist Guillermo Rosales, fleeing Castro's Cuba, was in Miami for just two days before he ended up in a boarding home that became the basis for his greatest work: *La Casa de Los Náufragos*, or *The Halfway House*. Another great Cuban, the poet Lorenzo García Vega, was co-founder of one of the most important literary journals of the 20th century, *Orígenes*. He also spent the last 10 years of his life in Miami working as a bag boy at a Publix supermarket. In wonderful late poems such as "By the Golf Course", Vega savages the empty materialism he sees all around him, even refusing to call Miami by name and instead referring to it as "Albino Beach".

Loving this place as a writer, a reader or, god forbid, an intellectual, means accepting that Miami doesn't love you back. Indeed, the most insightful fictional tale about modern Miami is a collection of stories about how to get out of it: Jennine Capó Crucet's *How to Leave Hialeah*. Until very recently, most smart kids who grew up here left. Miami is in the business of making Miami; the business of making art is still located in other places.

> "Miami is in the business of making Miami; the business of making art is still located in other places"

In its exiles in other cities you will nevertheless find a fierce, almost Stockholm Syndrome-like love for this city, which says a lot about the true meaning of literary Miami. For a writer there's something wonderful about a place that resists your efforts to pigeonhole it, to make it reflect your personal aesthetics. If Miami's fragmented, always-under-construction nature prevents more of a literary scene from forming, it provides something more valuable: a culture that isn't defined by the elite. Literary scene and literary culture aren't the same thing: a literary scene is any activity defined by curators, whereas literary culture cannot be so easily governed and controlled.

At El Palacio de los Jugos, a famous food market, I met a woman who was illiterate but composed poems in her head, memorised them and recited them aloud. Who gave her permission to do that? And where else in the US do half the children memorise the poetry of José Martí?

My hope for the "Literary Miami of the Future" – and there's always a "Miami of the Future" – is that it will stay wild and ungoverned, even as independent bookshops such as Books & Books and Miami Book Fair International continue to grow and newer organisations such as Bookleggers mobile library, Reading Queer, The Writer's Room at The Betsy Hotel and The Ashbery Home School find their audiences. I'd actually hate for Miami to end up like Paris. I was there for a week last year and I didn't hear a single poem. — (M)

ABOUT THE WRITER: P Scott Cunningham is a poet and translator. He is the founder and director of O, Miami Poetry Festival and the executive editor of Jai-Alai Books.

In with the old
Historical Miami

This is a city that embraces glitz and glamour. But it is increasingly recognising the value of preserving the past – which is why postcodes are appearing in once-neglected districts.

by Megan Cross Schmitt, preservation officer

As Miami races to establish itself as a leading global destination for all things shiny and new, there is a quiet renaissance taking place in some of the city's oldest neighbourhoods. Despite the current rapid rate of new development – and the obvious dangers this poses to anything deemed "outdated" – Miami's historic assets are turning heads thanks to a realisation that they can actually be good for development.

If this sounds like old news, that's because it is – throughout the rest of the world anyway. Examples of clever redevelopment include everything from The Limelight nightclub in New York, opened in a former Episcopal church built in 1845, to London's Tate Modern repurposing the abandoned Bankside Power Station to become one of the most important art galleries in the world. Miami, however, is a young city, only established in 1896. History shows us that it has long placed a premium on starting

out with a clean slate and such a mentality has created challenges for the preservation movement.

It is well known that a small group of dedicated activists helped to save the art deco buildings of South Beach in the late 1970s when they were in danger of being torn down. What is not so well known is the story of the many property-owners throughout Miami who, starting in the mid-1980s, took it upon themselves to seek historic-district status for their neighbourhoods in an effort to protect them from insensitive development.

Miami's first historic district, Morningside, was created in 1984; its most recent one, a small section of Little Havana called Riverview, was passed in the spring of 2015. Even now, in the midst of so much change, Miami's historic districts are an incredible way to experience some of the most surprising and enjoyable sides of the city, especially for architecture geeks.

The Spring Garden Historic District, established in 1997, is a jewel of lush foliage and eclectic buildings, situated on the Miami River where it meets the Seybold Canal. This little neighbourhood transports visitors back in time to when Miami was establishing itself as a newly developing city, all the while reinforcing the importance of waterways to its settlement patterns.

Just down the river from Spring Garden is the Lummus Park Historic District, established in 2004. Nowhere

Alternative Miami landmarks

01 Marjory Stoneman Douglas House
The renowned journalist and feminist's beautiful home.
02 Bacardi Building
Tropical, beautiful and confident – especially the annex.
03 Miami Marine Stadium
Brilliant representation of the recent past.

in Miami is it as hard to reconcile the proximity of the Central Business District with the sensation of being in a sleepy Southern residential neighbourhood. The district is also where one of Miami's most unique buildings can be found, the Scottish Rite Temple, making it worth the trip if only for that.

Today Miami's older neighbourhoods are some of the most sought-after areas in which to live and work. Recently much has been written about the Mimo/Biscayne Historic District. Perhaps nowhere more than here are the words "rebirth" and "renaissance" used to describe Miami's new love affair with its walkable, smaller-scale historic neighbourhoods. Now, thanks to some key players, this largely commercial historic district is home to some of the city's best new restaurants and bars, many of which are housed in the old, quirky and playful Mimo buildings that line Biscayne Boulevard. Miami's relatively new building regulation code, Miami21, promotes scale-appropriate, mixed-use, transport-oriented development. But savvy developers and natural-born urbanists realise that some of the city's best examples of such design already exist in our historic districts.

"Miamians increasingly crave experiences that allow them to connect with their history"

The Buena Vista East Historic District (BVEHD) is another section of Miami that is currently receiving attention thanks to its proximity to a glossy, buzzy neighbour to the south: the Design District. It's a luxury-shopping destination now home to the sort of edgy and exclusive boutiques that were once only found in the shopping malls just outside Miami. BVEHD, on the other hand, is a beautiful and lush residential area with a charming strip of small shops and cafés along Northeast 2nd Avenue between 42nd and 48th streets.

Walking its streets feels like a lesson in Miami's architectural styles and it is easy to see why this is the city's first neighbourhood to be declared a historic district. The stability and charm of BVEHD is protected: all changes to the buildings' exteriors, as well as new construction projects, require the approval of the City of Miami's Preservation Office and Historic and Environmental Preservation Board.

The appeal of heritage properties is not limited to specific districts though. Little by little within Downtown, smaller-scale projects are emerging too. The former City National Bank Building is transforming into the boutique Langford Hotel, while a former post office has been converted into the Miami Center for Architecture and Design, a beloved community resource that hosts exhibitions and lectures. As Miamians increasingly crave experiences that allow them to connect with their history in authentic ways, the city's significant spaces will stand out as platforms that can deliver on this demand.

Miami has always been a city that has understood the power of development. It is an exciting time to witness it come to the realisation that honouring its past may be a critical component to the success of its future. — (M)

ABOUT THE WRITER: Megan Cross Schmitt is the preservation officer for the City of Miami. She worked for three years as the special assistant to the executive director at the New York City Landmarks Preservation Commission before moving to South Florida in 2011.

ESSAY 09

Money talks
Property development

The 1920s saw Miami turned from swampy marshland to sought-after real estate. There was another building boom in the 2000s – and Al Capone made an appearance in between times.

by Paul S George, professor of history

One observer has pronounced Miami America's most beguiling city. Another insists that it is the new capital of Latin America and the Caribbean. It's more of a southern-hemisphere settlement than an American city, people say. Clearly, everyone agrees that Miami is an area rich in spectacle, glitz and notoriety but what few realise is that this area became the place it is today during the frenzied property boom of the 1920s. Since then it has never looked back, even when reeling from economic downturns, overwhelmed by refugees from the Caribbean and Latin America or traumatised by mob and cartel violence.

The prosperity of that era transformed a young frontier city into an emerging metropolitan area. It offered larger-than-life developers such as Carl Fisher, a brash Indianan with deep pockets, an opportunity to carve the resort known the world over as Miami Beach from swamp and mangroves. Or George Merrick, the cerebral son of a congregational minister, who gave us Coral Gables, a Mediterranean-styled community rightfully known as the City Beautiful. Meanwhile Glenn Curtiss, America's greatest early aviator and the possessor of the first pilot's licence ever issued in the US, developed three communities – Hialeah, Miami Springs and Opa-locka – from former Everglades swampland in the northwest sectors of the area.

The boom introduced cutting-edge marketing, involving celebrity pitchmen such as boxing champion Gene Tunney and politician William Jennings Bryan, as well as outlandish icons such as Rosie, Carl Fisher's elephant, who assisted building projects by wrapping her trunk around a board. It introduced slick advertising in its conjuring of Venice or America's historic Southwest in places such as Miami Shores and Miami Springs, whose building designs showcased the architecture of other places and even other times. The era brought large developers to the Miami area keen to cash in on the passion for housing amid a soaring population and associated property prices.

Finally, the boom tapped into America's entrepreneurial spirit with the attendant belief that anything is possible. This spawned the "binder boys":

"Boom-era neighbourhoods, now notable for their distinctive architecture and ethnic variety, are the principal focus for these visitors"

slick speculators who hailed from the northeast and blew into Miami in 1925 to buy and sell property on margin at huge mark-ups. Sensing the decline of the unchecked affluence by that summer they fled the area. That left it to more established residents, many of whom were teenagers who cast themselves in the same mould as they bought and sold property along the crowded confines of Flagler Street, Miami's central thoroughfare.

Miami's
evolving 'hoods
—
01 Wynwood
Known worldwide for its
murals and street art.
02 Design District
Home to many of the city's
high-end fashion houses.
03 Midtown
Popular restaurants and big
box stores.

The boom was about outrageous sums of money as new developments sold out within hours of going on the market, with millions of dollars changing hands and investors literally throwing money at developers. At his peak, George Merrick was worth between $75m and $100m but was destitute a few years later when the bubble burst.

Great festivals, parades, sports tournaments and celebrity-watching were characteristic of the era. Miami became a venue for film production with movie themes that were influenced by its subtropical ambience and madcap land speculation – think the Marx Brothers' *Cocoanuts*, which focused on slick speculators selling plots in boomtime Florida. The flouting of Prohibition and the city's proximity to the Bahamas and Cuba made it a prime entryway for booze too, bringing organised-crime figures such as Al Capone to Miami to oversee their operations here.

Fast-forward to the international city and tourist mecca of today. Nearly 15 million people visit Greater Miami annually and its glitz, glamour and wealth are on display more than ever. Boom-era neighbourhoods, now notable for their distinctive architecture and ethnic variety, are the principal focus for these visitors. From courthouses and cinemas to churches, the area's most singular buildings are from the 1920s. The nightlife, tourist attractions and festivals of today, like those of the earlier era, are

a major draw. Television, films and adverts are filmed in Miami on a regular basis.

The building booms of the early 2000s resemble, in their promotions, speculations and developmental by-products, those of previous years. However, they have been more sustainable through their insistence on larger down-payments on units purchased. As before, this activity has been driven by larger-than-life entrepreneurs. The behemoths that have arisen as a result place Miami third among the nation's densest skylines.

Though Al Capone, who symbolised lawlessness in that earlier era, has been gone for two thirds of a century, in the aftermath of his demise the area hosted enough mob figures to prompt former FBI head J Edgar Hoover to say that he could eliminate organised crime simply by rounding up all of the criminals who gathered on Collins Avenue and 23rd Street each winter. Later, the city weathered the rise of violent drug cartels overseeing the influx of illicit drugs from points south.

When tourists roam from neighbourhood to neighbourhood in Miami, taking in all that the Art Deco District, Coconut Grove, Brickell, Wynwood, Downtown, Coral Gables, Little Havana and the Design District offer, they are stepping on nearly a century of history. The recent past, with its madcap property-growth spurt and the attendant circuses surrounding it, has only embellished what was already there. — (M)

ABOUT THE WRITER: Paul S George is a professor of history at Miami-Dade College, Wolfson Campus. He also serves as historian to cultural institution HistoryMiami.

ESSAY 10

Miami nice
Improved reputation

———

Global perception may take a while to catch up (blame Tony Montana) but gone are the days when Miami was synonymous with crime. Now even its once-neglected areas are beginning to thrive.

by Liv Lewitschnik, Monocle

In the 1980s, Miami's drug wars made it the murder capital of the nation. In 1981 alone, 622 murders were committed in Miami-Dade County; such was the bloodshed that the coroner had to rent a freezer van to accommodate the overflow of bodies at the morgue. A year earlier, Miami had been the setting for three-day violent riots that left 18 people dead.

Now the scene is very different. These days Miami wouldn't even rank in the top 50 for murders in the US but the image of this tropical metropolis as Vice City still sticks, in no small part thanks to the way it has been portrayed in popular culture.

A 1983 remake of the 1932 mob film *Scarface*, featuring Al Pacino as the Cuban drug kingpin who runs his fearsome empire from Miami and goes out spectacularly in a shower of bullets, helped seal Miami's reputation. Then there was the crime series *Miami Vice* that ran between 1984 and 1989 and did much to develop the image of the lawless, pastel-shaded Miami in the public imagination. The arrival of the infamously violent video game *Grand Theft Auto* and its setting in Vice City, a fictional Miami, firmly fixed the concept of the city as a place of pimps, murderous gangs and daily shoot-outs between cars with tinted windows.

Though there is still truth to the image – shoot-outs do occasionally happen – Miami is a much safer place today. The 2013 murder rate stood at 71 per 100,000 people and community-based efforts to make Miami a better place are having a real impact. These efforts include an initiative launched by bike-shop owner Karim Nahim to give away new bicycles in exchange for guns in a bid to get weapons off the street. And for years authorities have successfully worked on getting people out of gangs and into jobs through the community-based programme Weed and Seed.

"These days Miami wouldn't even rank in the top 50 for murders in the US but the image of 'Vice City' still sticks"

The change in Miami goes all the way to the big art movers and shakers at Art Basel Miami Beach, who have helped put much dignity back into the city's image as it has jumped into the world spotlight for its cultural offerings. The creative influx has helped transform blighted areas as well. Just look at the murals adorning former industrial spaces in Wynwood or the growing list of galleries opening up in areas that were once deserted.

Wynwood is perhaps the most obvious example of Miami's image changing from dangerous to sleek – but with an edge still palpable. Young developers such as Tony Cho have played no small part in making Wynwood a place you ought to explore on your visit (see our neighbourhood walk on page 136).

Miami's most-talked about developer, Craig Robins, created the city's Design District and helped transform South Beach. Gorgeous people and, for the most part, beautifully renovated hotels abound in the sun-drenched area, as do police officers who are stationed just about everywhere here. It's probably the safest place in town.

Next on Miami's makeover list is Little Haiti, a poor neighbourhood of mostly Haitian immigrants down the road from Wynwood. Little Haiti is on the cusp of change: young people are beginning to renovate still relatively cheap property and open restaurants and shops here. Up-and-coming galleries such as the Yeelen Gallery are already doing brisk business and the neighbourhood has its own (still rare for Miami) organic farm and a newly opened co-working space.

Miami has come a long way from the violent days of the 1980s. Little Haiti's transformation from crime-ridden no-go area to must-see spot on any intrepid traveller's agenda is yet another example of how it is steadily moving away from the Vice City label while holding on to its gutsy identity. — (M)

ABOUT THE WRITER: Liv Lewitschnik is a MONOCLE contributing editor. Having grown up in the decidedly safe Swedish capital Stockholm, she now relishes the chance to get to live in the slightly more raucous Miami with her family.

ESSAY 11
Casting a spell
Miami's magic

If you can't beat 'em, join 'em. This city will never be tamed but armed with the following advice you'll be well placed to enjoy its wild side.

by Rob Goyanes, poet and critic

A Methodist minister and citrus farmer named EV Blackman coined Miami "The Magic City" in 1895, a year before the arrival of Henry Flagler's railroads and Miami's incorporation as a municipality. The name, given to describe its sudden appearance as a city without the preceding stage of "town", is a most fitting sobriquet, not only for the recurring truth of rapid development but also because Miami is a conjuror that plays with the idea of fantasy and reality. It offers both the illusion of paradise and paradise itself.

As a native I've learnt a lot of the tricks. Though obviously I can't reveal a magician's secrets

I can offer some ontological guidance in the form of five simple rules.

Rule 1: *Everything you think about Miami is simultaneously right and wrong.*
The city's reputation precedes it. Miami is imagined to be an oasis of beachfronts and parties, with a new world-class cultural scene. Indeed, the tropical wonders are like nothing else on the planet; there are endless options for eating, dancing and imbibing. And there's a flourishing art, music and literary community that is getting noticed the world over.

There's also the reputation of the shady underbelly: the vice and the vice economy, requisite of all megalopolises but acute in The Magic City. The sort of violence that pervaded the 1980s and helped to create that notorious image (and the accompanying film and TV shows) is old news. Miami has grown from that, though it has its struggles like any US city. However, transnational drug networks did lay down infrastructure for flows of global capital, high-rise development and diverse flocks of people. Our sordid history is ingrained in our culture, though by now we've mostly learnt to settle down and just reach for a *cafecito*.

Rule 2: *Nativity is relative.*
Miami is a place of exile. The further away your place of origin,

Magical locales
—
01 Bird Bowl
Historic, unpretentious bowling alley with great karaoke.
02 O, Miami
A poetry organisation that throws a festival in April.
03 Fruit and Spice Park
The only tropical botanical garden of its kind in the US.

the more at home you'll be. Cubans and Venezuelans and Haitians and countless other communities came to escape despots, poverty and bloodshed. A significant and diverse Jewish community started to settle here after the Second World War. Black history is entwined in the story of the city's railroads (and should be intrinsic to how the city builds its future). Miami is where celebrities go to step away from – or into – the spotlight and where families from the Midwest come to recklessly tan. Diversity reigns in this contemporary slice of the American Dream.

Plant and animal life adheres to this rule too. The tremendous panoply of flora is a mix of native and exotic species. Coastal mangroves and silver palms are indigenous, as is the dinosaurian alligator and American crocodile. Then there's the non-native: the towering Banyan trees and the evergreen Australian pines, both of which have a tendency to overrun native plant life. The landscape is a composition based on international travel, here by mandate, malintent or mistake.

Rule 3: *Keep it fluid.*

Geologically, the land of South Florida is a gargantuan, porous mound of fossilised sea life. The literal foundation upon which everything is built is constantly shifting. But this doesn't mean earthquakes or sinkholes: it means fluidity, a guiding principle of Miami. The city's development in the 19th century included an extensive canal system built to drain the Everglades. We have learnt the hard way that the water will always try to reassert itself and wind up causing flooding so now there's a massive mitigation project in place to try to return the Everglades to their original form.

> "Miami is where celebrities go to step away from – or into – the spotlight and where families from the Midwest come to recklessly tan"

To get the most out of Miami you need to explore wide and deep; keep the mind adrift. Rent a car to experience everything Miami-Dade County and beyond has to offer. Neighbourhood trolleys (buses that look like trams) and the Metrorail can help get you around within some neighbourhoods but a car is unfortunately your best ally. A boat is even better.

Rule 4: *Be sure to drive slowly in Coconut Grove.*

If while behind the wheel in this historic and lush neighbourhood you suddenly come to a line of traffic both ways, it most likely means there's a flock of kaleidoscopically winged peacocks making their way across the street. They arrived in the 1950s as pets of the wealthy; they've never left.

Rule 5: *Do not miss the greatest trick of all.*

With a rise of just a few degrees – meaning just a few feet of water – Miami may disappear entirely. The city has always lived at the edge of globalisation and it's here that the future of the world might just be played out, in economic, social and environmental terms. In 1987, TD Allman wrote a prescient book called *Miami: City of the Future*, so named because it exists as a portal. That's not only to Latin America but to the world that's beyond everything, the one we have yet to experience. This is the reason Miami is such a strange, wonderful and highly contemporary *ciudad*. In The Magic City, prophecy is the magician's most dazzling trick. — (M)

ABOUT THE WRITER: Rob Goyanes is a critic and poet from Miami. Born prematurely in the small town of Brooksville, Florida, he was helicoptered to a hospital in Gainesville, before settling in The Magic City. Goyanes writes for *Paris Review*, *Vice* and *Miami Rail* and runs Miami Music Club.

ESSAY 12
Court of appeal
Jai alai

Miami is no stranger to foreign influences but one of its most unexpected is a ball game from the Basque Country. Alas, jai alai's days look numbered – will the city take up the challenge of preserving it?

by Jason Li,
Monocle

Jai alai legends

01 Iñaki Osa Goikoetxea
The Spaniard is a nine-time world champion.
02 Benny Bueno
Retiring in 2005, Bueno was one of the world's best.
03 Leon Shepard
The only US-born athlete playing at the Miami Jai-Alai.

Take a look at the people and it's evident that fitness is an intrinsic part of Miami's DNA. When the 1985 ad campaign for Calvin Klein was shot atop the Breakwater Hotel on Ocean Drive, it was a celebration of South Beach's art deco architecture, sure, but the perfect forms of the nude models also tapped into the city's obsession with looking good. No wonder then that its fitness and cosmetic-surgery industries are booming.

Ironically, even as more barre studios and wellness centres spring up, a sad casualty of this quest for anatomical perfection is the demise of a sport known as jai alai. You haven't heard of it? Fear not. The game dates back four centuries to the Basque Country and was brought to the US in 1904, when Miami became the first place in the world to play the sport professionally. It resembles a kind of three-walled squash court but has an elongated basket called a *cesta*, which is used to catch the ball and promptly fling it back towards the wall.

Meaning "merry festival" in Basque, jai alai is known for its dizzying pace. In its heyday during the 1950s, thousands – including Ernest Hemingway, Harry Truman and Eleanor Roosevelt – flocked to fill the Miami Jai-Alai stadium (known as a fronton) to cheer on their favourite teams and athletes. In the 1960s, interest in the game warranted Miami Jai-Alai to undergo a million-dollar overhaul to accommodate the growing number of spectators.

Sadly, few were able to predict that after reaching its apex in the 1970s, mob influence, illicit gambling and other unsavoury elements would tarnish the sport's reputation. Frontons across the country pulled down their shutters. Today Miami Jai-Alai is a rare fronton in the US where the game is played year-round and is financially supported by the adjoining casino. The regulars who go nowadays are mostly in their sixties and seventies.

Once these old-timers are no more, jai alai's fate is uncertain. It has already become a sort of sentimental artefact and nostalgic plaything for the creative community. But before it becomes a relic, Miamians need to do more to make sure the state of jai alai is not allowed to further fade. Let's hope for future generations that they don't drop the ball. — (M)

ABOUT THE WRITER: Jason Li is MONOCLE's Toronto deputy bureau chief. He's hopped on and off countless fitness bandwagons but has recently settled on a surprisingly simple regime: a daily 5km run and some push-ups and sit-ups. Jai alai is yet to feature.

Culture
—— Inspiration
pointers

Miami didn't become one
of the world's top holiday
destinations because of
its cultural offerings. Its
allure, rather, lay in its
beach and the promise
of a mix of downtime
and sunset aperitifs.

Yet recently the
city has experienced
a cultural boom that
has transformed the
landscape. Miami's art
world has been catapulted
to international attention
and acclaim, especially
since Art Basel arrived
on its sandy shores
in 2002. The city has
also pioneered "the
Miami model", whereby
collectors publicly
showcase their art in
private galleries such
as the De la Cruz and the
Rubell Family Collection.

And while it may still
be in its adolescence
– Miami Beach was
alligator-infested
swampland until about
a century ago – the city
is more promising and
dynamic than ever thanks
to its growing number of
museums, cinemas and
music venues. So, as fun
as it is to top up the tan,
there's no excuse not to
see and do more.

Cinemas
Picture perfect

①
O Cinema, Wynwood
Cinephile centre

This 112-seat independent venture,
which screens documentaries, indie
and foreign films, is hard to miss
with its bright-pink door and retro
neon sign. Cinephiles are spoilt for
choice: there's a film library and
shop, as well as a snack counter.

On balmy evenings it hosts
Cine Al Fresco screenings in the
courtyard and there are regular
themed dinner-and-movie nights
with chef Michael Schwartz of
Harry's Pizzeria. The non-profit
cinema has other branches in
Miami Beach and Miami Shores
but this is the finest.
90 Northwest 29th Street, 33127
+1 305 571 9970
o-cinema.org

②
Tower Theater, Little Havana
Festival favourite

Tower Theater opened in 1926
as one of the city's first picture
houses and was later a mainstay
among Cuban émigrés seeking
out Spanish-language films. It
was out of action for 18 years
until Miami Dade College (MDC)
brought it back to life and now
shows a mix of independent
Spanish and English-language films.

The cinema also hosts cultural
events and MDC lectures, and is
a regular Miami International Film
Festival venue. Ball & Chain (*see
page 46*) across the road is handy
for tapas and rum after the show.
1508 Southwest 8th Street, 33135
+1 305 237 2463
towertheatermiami.com

Wheel deal

Blue Starlite Mini Urban
Drive-In brings a little bit of
the old-school American
experience back to the city.
Enjoy a slider basket while
singing along to 'Grease' and,
say organisers, "feel free to
make out in your car".
miamiurbandrivein.com

③
Coral Gables Art Cinema, Coral Gables
Indie hit

This 141-seat venue was opened in 2010 by Steven Krams to bring independent and international features, regional premieres, documentaries and classics to a Miami audience. The programme is ably scheduled by Nat Chediak, co-founder of the Miami International Film Festival, with the latest art-house releases on offer as well as free screenings of classics.

There's also no shortage of gourmet snacks, such as Peterbrooke handmade chocolates, Dolci Peccati gelato and Spanish wines.
260 Aragon Avenue, 33134
+1 786 385 9689
gablescinema.com

Oh, I thought this was a 3D monocle

④
Miami Beach Cinematheque, South Beach
Social screenings

No art-house venue compares to the Cinematheque in the historic former South Beach City Hall, built by Carl Fisher in 1927. It is now home to the Miami Beach Film Society, started by film connoisseur Dana Keith – who also opened this cosy cinema in 2003.

The 50-seat screening room shows documentaries alongside foreign and independent films, and showcases premieres from international film festivals. An art gallery, bookshop and small café complete this cinematic delight.
1130 Washington Avenue, 33139
+1 305 673 4567
mbcinema.com

Miami on screen

01 Miami Vice, 1984-1989:
This five-season TV cop show transformed the city's reputation and helped its pastel art deco architecture (and Don Johnson's rolled-sleeves Armani-jacket look) reach a global audience.

02 Scarface, 1983:
Al Pacino's performance as Cuban drug lord Tony Montana is unforgettable, even if quoting his "Say hello to my little friend" line is getting a touch old.

03 A Hole in the Head, 1959:
Another Tony, this time played by Frank Sinatra, takes the stage as a widowed hotel proprietor in Frank Capra's comedy-drama that shows off Miami's beautiful sights.

Theatres
Dramatic high

①
Miami Light Project at Goldman Warehouse, Wynwood
Eclectic power

This performing-arts theatre stages plays, music and dance acts as well as interactive film events at the Goldman Warehouse.

The non-profit cultural organisation is not only there to entertain: it also promotes South Florida talent in and around Miami, having commissioned more than 75 artists since its foundation in 1989. From plays by Edinburgh Fringe award-winners to jazz performances and indie film nights, Miami Light Project has played a major part in developing the city's cultural legacy.
404 Northwest 26th Street, 33127
+1 305 576 4350
miamilightproject.com

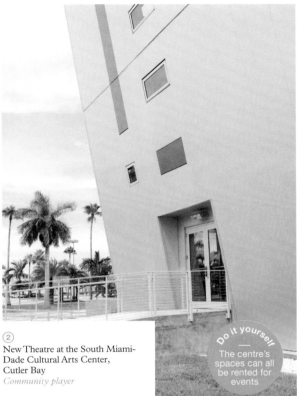

②
New Theatre at the South Miami-
Dade Cultural Arts Center,
Cutler Bay
Community player

This multicultural theatre company
is housed in the arts centre that was
built in 2011 to revitalise Cutler Bay
after the destruction wrought by
Hurricane Andrew. It is well worth
the 30-minute drive from the centre
of Miami. The New Theatre puts
on works by Pulitzer Prize-winning
playwrights and brings classic and
contemporary plays to the stage.

"We're the small theatre that
can," says artistic director Ricky J
Martinez, who champions Miamian
playwrights reflecting on social and
cultural issues in South Florida.
The theatre is also known for its
revival of major pieces that pack out
the intimate venue, such as Arthur
Miller's *Death of a Salesman*. "It's all
about connecting with people."
*South Miami-Dade Cultural Arts
Center, 10950 Southwest 211 Street,
33189*
+1 786 573 5300
new-theatre.org

Do it yourself
—
The centre's
spaces can all
be rented for
events

①
Museum of Contemporary Art,
North Miami
Modern provocateur

American conceptual artist John
Baldessari, minimalist Dan Flavin,
the versatile Dennis Oppenheim
and Tokyo-born Mariko Mori
are just a few of the artists whose
work is part of Moca's 600-piece
permanent collection.

The museum, known for
its provocative and innovative
exhibitions, was founded as the
Center of Contemporary Art in
1981 before moving into Charles
Gwathmey and Jose Gelabert-
Navia's spectacular build in North
Miami in 1996. The institution's
most popular past exhibitions
have encompassed illustrious
shows from Roy Lichtenstein
to Bruce Weber. It's also worth
swinging by the free outdoor jazz
concerts held on the last Friday
of every month.
*Joan Lehman Building, 770
Northeast 125th Street, 33161*
+1 305 893 6211
mocanomi.org

②
Wolfsonian-FIU, South Beach
Designs for life

The Wolfsonian's gold-and-green
glazed-terracotta fountain in
the entrance hall is the star of
Miami's Art Deco District and
hints at the eclectic collection
of more than 150,000 objects
within the museum's walls. The
institution, which belongs to
Florida International University,
was founded in 1986 to exhibit
and preserve Mitchell Wolfson Jr's
collections; today it is a museum,
library and research centre.

Particularly impressive is its
permanent *Art and Design in the
Modern Age* exhibition, which
displays 19th to 20th-century
memorabilia. Especially noteworthy
are the vintage propaganda posters,
in addition to the cameras, clocks
and radios designed as part of
the American Industrial Design
movement by the likes of Walter
Dorwin Teague and John Vassos.
1001 Washington Avenue, 33139
+1 305 531 1001
wolfsonian.org

Green foundation

In 2016, the Patricia and
Phillip Frost Museum of
Science moves into a new
$300m Grimshaw Architects-
designed home in Museum
Park. The sustainable
new building includes a
planetarium and aquarium.
miamisci.org

Extra insight

Tag along
on the free
guided tour
on Fridays

③

Pérez Art Museum Miami,
Downtown
Thematic thinking

This modern- and contemporary-
art museum, initially established
as the Center for Fine Arts in
1984, has a magnificent new
Herzog & de Meuron-designed
home in Museum Park, where it
moved in 2013. The three-storey
building overlooking Biscayne
Bay is sheltered by a leafy canopy
created by botanist Patrick Blanc.
Inside, six thematic galleries and
three more focused ones show
thought-provoking artwork drawn
from the museum's 1,800-piece
collection, which is heavy on US,
Latin American and African art.
There are also special exhibitions
by renowned artists such as
Ai Weiwei and José Bedia. On
a sunny day, loll on Konstantin
Grcic's Netscape swinging-chair
installation or head to Stephen
Starr's Verde restaurant terrace.
1103 Biscayne Boulevard, 33132
+1 305 375 3000
pamm.org

④

Bass Museum, South Beach
Classic contemporary

This museum was named in honour
of John and Johanna Bass, whose
donation of Renaissance and
Baroque art is the backbone of its
collection. It also showcases textiles,
tapestries and artefacts dating from
the 7th to the 20th century, and
21st-century North American, Latin
American, Asian and Caribbean art.
   Its treasures are nestled within
Russell Pancoast's 1930s art deco
landmark, once the Miami Beach
Library and Art Center. Fifty
years after opening its doors, the
Bass is expanding and will reopen
in autumn 2016. Until then, the
museum has launched BassX, a
series of solo artist projects, talks,
and events, held in a pop-up
gallery space across the street in
the Miami Beach Regional Library
(227 22nd Street).
2100 Collins Avenue, 33139
+1 305 673 7530
bassmuseum.org

⑤

Institute of Contemporary
Art, Miami, Design District
Culture club

The ICA Miami has found
itself a new home in the Design
District. Currently located in

a temporary gallery space in
the historic Moore Building
constructed in 1921, the Institute
will be moving into a brand-new
venue designed by Madrid-based
studio Aranguren & Gallegos
in December 2016.
   The exhibition hall and
extensive sculpture garden
will give the ICA Miami a bigger
platform to engage with the public
and showcase the work of artists
such as Andra Ursuta, John Miller,
Virginia Overton and Ryan
Sullivan. Exhibitions by these and
other artists already reflect the
museum's ongoing commitment
to confronting audiences with
the most experimental of
contemporary works.
4040 Northeast 2nd Avenue, 33137
+1 305 901 5272
icamiami.org

I call this one,
'Miami in the
Present'. It's a
layered piece

Private collections
Miami models

①
Craig Robins Collection,
Design District
Estate of the art

This is a singular art collection.
Not only because it includes
pieces by Marlene Dumas,
John Baldessari, Richard Tuttle
and Paul McCarthy but because
its 1,000 items are displayed in
the office of Craig Robins's
property firm Dacra. Pieces
by Jean Prouvé and Konstantin
Grcic furnish the purpose-built
space, where staff are surrounded
by sculptures, canvases and
installations such as British artist
Stuart Haygarth's spherical
creation "Tide".

"There is nothing that I have
as a work of art or piece of design
that I don't want to share," says
Robins, whose collection is open
by appointment only. "I see myself
more as a custodian, holding onto
it and caring for it."
Dacra, 3841 Northeast 2nd Avenue,
Suite 400, 33137
+1 305 531 8700
dacra.com

②
Rubell Family Collection,
Wynwood
Big names in store

"We don't pick art: art picks us,"
says Donald Rubell, who began
collecting art with his wife Mera in
New York. Together they established
their collection in 1964 and
relocated to Miami in 1993.

Housed in a former Drug
Enforcement Agency warehouse
for confiscated goods, RFC is one of
the world's largest privately owned
contemporary-art collections. It
contains works by international
artists such as Cady Noland, Cindy
Sherman, Anselm Kiefer, Charles
Ray and Keith Haring.
95 Northwest 29th Street, 33127
+1 305 573 6090
rfc.museum

③
De la Cruz Collection
Contemporary Art Space,
Design District
Family affair

In 2009, Rosa and Carlos de la
Cruz opened a gallery in the Design
District to showcase their growing
private collection, which was
previously on display in their home.

Their space was designed in
collaboration with John Marquette
and focuses on American
abstraction, with works by Wade
Guyton, Kelley Walker and Sterling
Ruby. "Our building allows viewers
to have their own interpretation
of the collection based on their
personal experience," says Rosa.
23 Northeast 41st Street, 33137
+1 305 576 6112
delacruzcollection.org

Commercial galleries
Art market

① **Fredric Snitzer Gallery, Downtown**
Next big things

Fredric Snitzer's space is known for its leading role in the contemporary-art scene and brings international attention to emerging and mid-career artists such as Hernan Bas, Alexander Kroll and Naomi Fisher.

Snitzer spent close to 10 years in Wynwood before relocating further south when that neighbourhood became too commercial for him. His gallery exhibits an impressive collection of art, including pieces by installation artists Alice Aycock and Rafael Domenech, Cuban photographer María Martínez-Cañas and Argentine artist Diego Singh.
1540 Northeast Miami Court, 33132
+1 305 448 8976
snitzer.com

FREDRIC SNITZER

Plain view
—
The minimal black exterior is hard to miss

②
David Castillo, South Beach
Cultural identity

"My gallery has a particular vision and we show a balance between internationally known artists and local artists I have fostered since the gallery's inception," says David Castillo of his eponymous South Beach gallery, founded 11 years ago. His exhibitions possess a historical, social and cultural depth and show work by the likes of Louise Bourgeois, Jean-Michel Basquiat, Marcel Duchamp, Wifredo Lam, Pablo Picasso, Sigmar Polke and Andy Warhol.

Among the artists that Castillo himself looks after are Sanford Biggers, Kate Gilmore, Jose Lerma, Xaviera Simmons and Shinique Smith. "All 20 of my artists are representative of the gallery's aesthetic and vision, which deals primarily with identity – be it cultural, personal or art-historical," he says.
420 Lincoln Road, 33139
+1 305 573 8110
davidcastillogallery.com

③
Gallery Diet, Wynwood
Conceptual pioneer

"As a native of Miami it was
quite exciting to see the cultural
renaissance our city was
experiencing in the early 2000s,"
says Nina Johnson-Milewski,
who founded Wynwood's Gallery
Diet in 2007. "I truly felt that if
I opened in Miami I would be
contributing something of value
to the community."

The contemporary-art gallery
puts on about nine shows a year
by local and international artists
such as Emmett Moore, Betty
Woodman, Rochelle Feinstein
and Nicolas Lobo. Work such
as Lobo's socio-critical solo
show *Bad Soda/Soft Drunk* is
emblematic of Diet's conceptually
rigorous exhibitions. "We don't
just participate in a 'local' scene
but rather function as a porthole
to the international art world,"
says Johnson-Milewski.
174 Northwest 23rd Street, 33127
+1 305 571 2288
gallerydiet.com

④
Dina Mitrani Gallery, Wynwood
Visual poetry

Miamian Dina Mitrani opened
her photography gallery in 2008
in what had been her parents'
clothing factory for 40 years. The
space lends itself to exhibitions
with a personal touch, such as
Peggy Levison Nolan's *Anonymous:
The Fractured Histories of Found
Photographs*, featuring a collection
of lost-and-found early photographs
displayed salon-style.

"I am working on continuing
to define my programme, leaning
towards narrative and conceptual
work with a poetic undertone and
a final aesthetic that gets me in the
gut," says Mitrani, who has shown
work by photographers such as
Marina Font, Roberto Huarcaya
and Thomas Jackson. While you're
here, it's worth heading next door to
Mitrani's sister Rhonda's video-art
gallery The Screening Room. It's
a family affair.
2620 Northwest 2nd Avenue, 33127
+1 786 486 7248
dinamitranigallery.com

⑤
Spinello Projects, Allapattah
Rebellious nature

Anthony Spinello's experimental,
one-of-a-kind gallery and creative
platform showcases art of every
conceivable medium by emerging
Miami talent, as well as international
names. It has become a bastion for
unorthodox artists who aren't fond
of traditional galleries.

Some of the names on Spinello's
books include Miamians Antonia
Wright and Typoe, Buenos Aires-
born Agustina Woodgate, Israeli
Naama Tsabar, Nicaragua-born
Farley Aguilar and French duo
Abby Double. Whenever you drop
by, prepare to be surprised.
2930 Northwest 7th Avenue, 33127
+1 786 271 4223
spinelloprojects.com

Art in public

Miami is dotted with work by
world-class artists, architects
and designers. Miami Beach
set up Art in Public Places in
1984, which reserves 1.5 per
cent of city hall's building-
programmes budget to be
spent on public art.
miamidadepublicart.org

 Alejandra von Hartz Gallery, Wynwood
Abstract expression

This space explores geometric abstraction, constructivism, minimalism and conceptual art. Many of the artists here, including Pablo Siquier, Karina Peisajovich, Teresa Pereda, Amadeo Azar and Juan Pablo Garza, have South and Latin American roots. The other side of the pond is represented by artists such as London-based Sam Winston.

Past exhibitions have revolved around the relationship between art, architecture and space and have thrown a light on the globalisation of the contemporary-art world.
2630 Northwest 2nd Avenue, 33127
+1 305 438 0220
alejandravonhartz.net

Staying power — This gallery has been around since 2002

7 Tub Gallery Miami, Wynwood
Revolutionary spirit

Architect Miguel Fernández opened Tub to introduce international artists such as Brazilian Cristina Barroso and Cuban Jorge Wellesley to a local audience.

The name comes from Jacques-Louis David's 18th-century painting "The Death of Marat", which shows the French revolutionary expiring in his bathtub between inkpot and letters; in this allegory, the tub is the space where ideas are born. The venue also hosts Q&A sessions with artists, curators, designers and collectors.
3801 North Miami Avenue 101, 33127
+1 786 663 2548
tubgallerymiami.com

8 Locust Projects, Design District
Experimental space

Miami-based artists Elizabeth Withstandley, Westen Charles and Bryan Cooper founded Locust Projects in a converted warehouse to give artists a platform for their ambitious ventures. "We are dedicated to providing contemporary visual artists with the freedom to experiment with new ideas without the pressures of gallery sales or the limitations of conventional exhibition spaces," says Chana Sheldon, Locust Projects' executive director.

Artists whose work is displayed here include Kate Gilmore, Francesca DiMattio, Jim Drain, Agustina Woodgate, Ruben Ochoa, Theaster Gates, Daniel Arsham and Jillian Mayer. In autumn 2014, Locust launched Art on the Move, a public-art initiative that places specially commissioned projects around the city.
3852 North Miami Avenue, 33127
+1 305 576 8570
locustprojects.org

⑨
Dot Fiftyone Gallery, Wynwood
Creative communal

Dot Fiftyone Gallery was opened
by Alfredo Guzman and Isaac
Perelman in 2003 with the
vision of uniting artists with
Wynwood's community, even
before it became a developed arts
district. The institution is known
widely for championing emerging
homegrown and international
talent and for being a laboratory
for conceptual art.

Shows by artists such as
Eduardo Capilla, Raquel Schwartz,
Hernán Cédola, Mauro Giaconi
and Marcos Castro are to the
point, often concerned with erasing
geographical boundaries and
cultural gaps; that's one reason
Guzman and Perelman regularly
invite international resident artists
into the space. The gallery's
programming also incorporates
workshops, lectures, events and
philanthropic projects.
187 Northwest 27th Street, 33127
+1 305 573 9994
dotfiftyone.com

Music venues
Miami sounds

①
Grand Central Miami, Downtown
Multi-space station

This mid-sized club, housed in a
refitted railway station, hosts indie
bands, DJs and events such as
George Dawes Green's live
storytelling series The Moth.

If you're looking for something
more intimate, leave the warehouse
club behind and ascend the
staircase to The Garret, which feels
almost like a private loft and is the
place to hear Miami-based bands
play. International artists usually hit
the stage in the main room, which
has a superb sound system and
plenty of space for you to cut
shapes on the dance floor.
697 North Miami Avenue, 33136
+1 305 377 2277
grandcentralmiami.com

Brit abroad

Churchill's Pub in Little Haiti
is where locals and the
musically minded have been
meeting since 1979. The
institution, modelled on a UK
pub (except possibly divier),
is the place to enjoy live
rock and jazz music.
churchillspub.com

②
Olympia Theater at Gusman
Center, Downtown
Historic style

The Olympia Theater, designed
by John Eberson, opened as a
picture palace and Vaudeville
house in 1926 (it also attained
fame as the first air-conditioned
building in the South). With its
turrets and baroque balconies, the
theatre's interior evokes the set of
Shakespeare's *Romeo and Juliet* and
the Mediterranean style gives it an
old-world flair that is all too rare in
young Miami.

Philanthropist Maurice Gusman
saved the theatre from demolition
in 1975 and it was restored by
architect Morris Lapidus before
being listed on the National Register
of Historic Places in 1984. Where
once Etta James and Elvis rocked
the stage, the likes of Sufjan Stevens
and Kraftwerk play today. There
are also film screenings and free live
jazz nights.
174 East Flagler Street, 33131
+1 305 374 2444
olympiatheater.org

Walk-on part
—
The original
1926 carpet
was faithfully
recreated

Stretch out
—
Miami Beach
Soundscapes
shows free
films

Adrienne Arsht Center for
the Performing Arts, Downtown
Big noise

This 5,000-seat space designed by
architect Cesar Pelli is one of the
largest performing-arts complexes
in the country and is also where
the Miami City Ballet and the
Florida Grand Opera take to the
stage. Most big shows touring the
US make their first stop in Miami
at this Downtown venue, which
opened in 2006.

Order a pre-show dinner at chef
Allen Susser's The Café at Books
& Books in the landmark Carnival
Tower, before taking a seat in
Miami's performing-arts hub.
1300 Biscayne Boulevard, 33132
+ 1 305 949 6722
arshtcenter.org

⑤

The Fillmore Miami Beach at Jackie
Gleason Theater, South Beach
Star-studded heritage

Frank Sinatra and Bob Hope
were regulars in the audience in
the era when Jackie Gleason made
TV history here (no wonder the
1950-designed theatre was named
after the American comedy star).
From *The Ed Sullivan Show* to
performances by Liza Minelli
and St Vincent, the art deco
Fillmore has seen it all.

In 2007, the 3,500-seat theatre
became Florida's branch of Live
Nation's Fillmore music-venue
franchise, which made Janis Joplin
and Jefferson Airplane household
names. With its chandeliers and
slanted floor (so that even fans
at the back can catch a glimpse of
the stage), the Fillmore may not be
able to compete in size but it has
heaps more character than Miami's
mega-stadiums – over which we'd
pick it every time.
1700 Washington Avenue, 33139
+ 1 305 673 7300
fillmoremb.com

③
New World Center,
South Beach
Noted performances

This Miami Beach venue, designed
by Frank Gehry, hosts concerts,
broadcasts live music and shows
films and video art on its outdoor
projection wall.

Even if you're not into classical
music, it's a treat to see the building
lit up at night. It's even better
when you can enjoy a live Wallcast
performance, or a film as part of
the Arts in the Parks cinema series,
over a picnic under palms and
pergolas in the park designed by
Dutch urban-design and landscape-
architecture firm West 8.
500 17th Street, 33139
+ 1 305 673 3330
nws.edu

Media round-up
Word on the street

①
Newsstands, citywide
Print in the city

Five years ago it would have been difficult to find a copy of the Sunday *New York Times* but although the city still lacks specialist newsstands, there are now a few fine purveyors of print for your daily dose of global headlines.

The most dependable is **①** *News Café*, which has been around since 1988. Open 24 hours, seven days a week, this quaint pavement café, restaurant, bar and newsstand at the corner of 8th Street and Ocean Drive has all the titles you'll need during your stay. Peruse the latest *New Yorker* over a martini or digest *Vanity Fair* with your poached red snapper.

If you're looking for niche titles, head to Lincoln Road's **②** *Alchemist* and **③** *Base*. For the best selection of international press, don't miss **④** *Books & Books* on Aragon Avenue in Coral Gables.

TOP PICKS
01 News Café
800 Ocean Drive, 33139
+ 1 305 538 6397
newscafe.com

02 Alchemist
111 Lincoln Road, 33139
+ 1 305 531 4815
shopalchemist.com

03 Base
927 Lincoln Road, 33139
+ 1 305 531 4982
baseworld.com

04 Books & Books
265 Aragon Avenue, 33134
+ 1 305 442 4408
booksandbooks.com

②
Essential reading
Miami's best mags

With a series of new publications, Miami is finally stepping out of the shadows. "The city has become a beacon for entrepreneurs and creatives who see endless potential in what was once a resort town," says Tali Jaffe, **①** *Cultured* magazine's executive editor.

The art-and-design journal is published by Whitehaus Media Group and was joined on newsstands in 2012 by **②** *Miami Rail*, the free sibling of New York's *Brooklyn Rail*. For the literary-minded there's P Scott Cunningham's **③** *Jai-Alai Magazine*, a trove of poetry, fiction, essays and illustrations founded in 2011.

Monocle 24

For a global perspective, there is Monocle's own digital radio station M24. Keep up with the arts-and-media landscape with Robert Bound's weekly *Culture Show* and hear *The Stack's* take on the world of print with hosts Tyler Brûlé and Tom Edwards.
monocle.com/radio

Radio: Miami on the airwaves

01 **WLRN:** South Florida's public radio at 91.3FM has been on the air since 1948. Tune in to *Morning Edition* and *All Things Considered* in partnership with *The Miami Herald*.
wlrn.org

02 **WDNA:** At 88.9FM, this is South Florida's number-one jazz station. Don't miss *Passing Notes*, Friday's commentary on books and music.
wdna.org

03 **Planted in Miami:** This iTunes-listed podcast spotlights the businesses, artists and musicians who are raising the city's profile.
plantedinmiami.com

04 **Biscayne Tales:** This is a young city but there's plenty of history here, as this podcast reveals. Trace the footsteps of Carl Fisher, Miami's founding father, and discover the best landmarks to visit.
biscaynetales.com

Design and architecture
—— Eye candy

To think that the all-powerful developers wanted to tear it down at one point; thankfully it survived. We are of course talking about the Art Deco District in South Beach, the highest concentration of buildings of its kind in the world. But there is so much more to Miami than this, from historic Miami modern (Mimo) buildings – many of which are starting to get restored à la South Beach – to flamboyant "eclectic" styles, via a genuine contemporary desire to create the city's first urban core and ensure that it's beautiful at the same time.

Miami may be changing in swift fashion – which inevitably means constant construction – but people are taking an aesthetic approach to everything, from car parks to manhole covers, making the city one of the best places in the US for architecture and design buffs. And that's before we've even mentioned the museums, the design shows, the big-shot developers and the "starchitects".

Art deco buildings
20th-century style

1
Scottish Rite Temple,
Lummus Park
Eagle eye

This is the temple of the Scottish Rite of Freemasons – yes, those gentlemen with distinct hats and secret handshakes – but they're a terribly nice bunch and more than happy for you to come and see their impressive building. This Egyptian-inspired edifice was completed in 1924 in a style that would soon be known as art deco; the term wasn't officially coined until 1925.

The building, which cost about $350,000 to construct at the time, is marked by a set of four imposing Doric columns outside and above it four double-headed eagles that signify equality. Inside, where restoration was only recently completed, the 1,000-seater auditorium – the freemasons regularly teach through plays – is equally impressive.
471 Northwest 3rd Street, 33128
+1 305 374 4700
srmiami.org

②

United States Post Office,
South Beach
Stamp of approval

Built in 1937 by architect Howard
Lovewell Cheney, this is a prime
example of the art deco-offshoot
Depression moderne, a sub-style that
was used for a more sombre aesthetic
suited to public buildings.

As impressive as the outside is, the
interior is also outstanding: it features
three murals of "Episodes from the
History of Florida" painted in 1940
by artist Charles Russell Hardman.
The painted sun-like ceiling in the
entrance hall is especially captivating;
be sure to check out the 48-point
starburst around it.
1300 Washington Avenue, 33119
+1 305 672 2447
usps.com

Fancy that
——
In the 1980s, Miami Beach was
a crumbling retirement home
and its art deco buildings were
under threat. The renaissance
came with Leonard Horowitz's
movement to give buildings a
facelift by painting them pastel
colours – a palette that
endures to this day.

To the letter
——
The perfect
delivery of
depression
moderne

A good hand
—
The banister at Winter Haven is original

⑤
11th Street Diner, South Beach
Shake a leg

It's remarkable that quite possibly the finest example of streamline moderne (a late manifestation of art deco) in the whole of Miami Beach comes in the form of a shiny stainless steel, aluminium and glass diner. The dining car was constructed in 1948 by the Paramount Dining Car Company of Haledon, New Jersey. It spent more than 40 years of its life in Wilkes-Barre, Pennsylvania, before being dismantled and transported south to Miami where it reopened its doors in 1992.

It's a little bit of a tourist trap but it has remarkably well-preserved art deco flourishes in the interior, including the original light fixtures, which means you'll find the perfect excuse for propping yourself up at the bar with a Stunt Devil burger and peanut-butter milkshake.
1065 Washington Avenue, 33139
+1 305 534 6373
eleventhstreetdiner.com

④
The Essex House, South Beach
Look sharp

Designed by Henry Hohauser in 1938, this is one of the few South Beach art deco buildings that is still painted all white, as it would have appeared when it was first built. The strongest external feature is its central column – a key part of art deco design – with an almost rocket-ship-like shaft.

But it's inside the lobby at the terrazzo flooring that you need to look: three arrows at feet-level signify that there was once an illegal gambling den here. Also make sure you check out the famous painting above the fireplace of "Indians in the Everglades" by Earl Le Pan; he apparently wasn't allowed to include crocodiles when he originally made the piece as the owners thought it would scare guests. When he retouched the painting in the 1990s, he added the crocs.
1001 Collins Avenue, 33139
+1 305 534 2700
essexhotel.com

③
Winter Haven, South Beach
Straight edge

Ocean Drive may attract the hordes but it also contains the most concentrated number of art deco buildings in the world. Winter Haven, designed by architect Albert Anis in the 1930s, is one such gem: an example of streamline moderne – meaning curved as opposed to straight lines in the "eyebrows" above the windows – with ziggurat shapes around the top of the central column.

It's also worth stepping inside. The stairs leading up to the first floor have handrails – complete with glass balls – that are all original too.
1400 Ocean Drive, 33139
+1 305 531 5571
winterhavenhotelsobe.com

Does this count as a dining car if I eat a burger in it?

Car parks
Get in gear

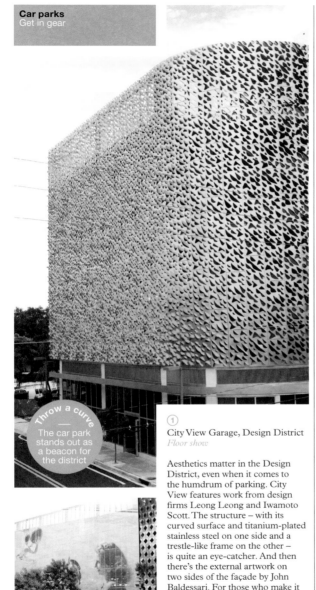

Throw a curve — The car park stands out as a beacon for the district

① City View Garage, Design District
Floor show

Aesthetics matter in the Design District, even when it comes to the humdrum of parking. City View features work from design firms Leong Leong and Iwamoto Scott. The structure – with its curved surface and titanium-plated stainless steel on one side and a trestle-like frame on the other – is quite an eye-catcher. And then there's the external artwork on two sides of the façade by John Baldessari. For those who make it to the roof? Colourful floor artwork from Island Planning Corporation.
Northeast 38th Street, between Northeast 1st Avenue and North Miami Avenue, 33137
miamidesigndistrict.com

② Bentley Bay Condominiums, South Beach
Land ho!

Bentley Bay was designed by Miami-based Arquitectonica, the company behind the redevelopment of Brickell. The car park is made of reinforced concrete and contains a trellis of metal poles, incorporating plants to give it a natural feel.
    The garage is part of a two-tower bayside complex of condominiums. The building was envisioned as a series of three sails: its ends are made concave or convex by the elevation of the balconies, creating the illusion that wind is the source of the sculptural distortion. The three "sails" are set as if leaving port towards the Caribbean.
520 West Avenue, 33139
arquitectonica.com

Stacked in style
—
The craze for designer car parks shows no sign of abating. Zaha Hadid is the latest starchitect to descend on the city with an ambitious curved structure in Collins Park Place, Miami Beach. Cars may dominate here but at least they're tucked away nicely.

1111 Lincoln Road, South Beach
Space invaders

Nowhere has the idea of a car park been elevated to an art form quite like it has in Miami. Interestingly this one, designed by Herzog & de Meuron, chooses to almost make the cars the centrepiece: the walls of the construction are open, allowing passers-by clear views of the motors parked inside (the architects call the design concept "all muscle without cloth"). Add to the angular support columns some great lighting, an in-house designer store called Atrium (*see page 49*), as well as a restaurant on its roof called Juvia, and you have a very Miami take on a car park.
1691 Michigan Avenue, 33139
1111lincolnroad.com

④ Park@420, South Beach
Glimmers of hope

This public car park opened towards the end of 2011, built atop a ground-floor retail space. New York firm Ten Arquitectos, headed by Enrique Norten, spotted an opportunity to create a structure that was contemporary while also paying homage to Miami's modernist architecture.

This was created with a precast concrete façade and a pattern of small openings that were formed to modulate light and shadow. At night this creates a jewel-like effect from the light of moving cars and the interior itself.
420 Lincoln Road (garage at 16th and Drexel Avenue), 33139
420lincolnroad.com

⑤ Fly's Eye Dome, Design District
Buck stops here

Buckminster Fuller, the celebrated US architect who died in 1983, designed and patented his Fly's Eye Dome in 1965. He built a set of prototypes by hand in 1977 but died before he was able to create a permanent structure. In 2011, Craig Robins – the developer behind the Design District – acquired a prototype and decided to build one in homage to Fuller. The reason we're telling you all of this? It now forms the rather lovely, space-age-like access to the district's second main car park via a spiral staircase (this one underground).
140 Northeast 39th Street, 33137
miamidesigndistrict.com

I will go to great lengths to find a parking space

Mimo buildings
Modern marvels

The Vagabond Hotel,
Mimo District
Taking root

This lovingly restored Mimo building
is a hotel and restaurant that opened
in 2014. Developer Avra Jain's
mission was to stay true to the original
abandoned hotel; a new sign (in a
retro style) and colourful rooms give
a kitsch mid-century modern
playfulness to the property.

There is great attention to detail,
as seen with the painstakingly restored
mermaid mosaic at the bottom of the
pool. Jain has her sights set elsewhere
too, developing the Miami River Inn:
part of a set of timber houses from
the start of the 20th century.
*7301 Biscayne Boulevard, 33138
+1 305 400 8420
thevagabondhotel.com*

Andiamo (former General Tire
Building), Mimo District
Pedal to the metal

It looks a little like a modernist petrol
station. In fact this building – now a
pizza restaurant – was built as the
Miami General Tire Building in 1954.
The architect was one of Mimo's
greatest, Robert Law Weed, then with
Weed Russell Johnson Associates.

Weed was behind landmarks such
as the Shrine Building – also on
Biscayne Boulevard – and the
University of Miami campus in Coral
Gables. Here he created a glass, steel
and concrete structure with a vast
overlay roof and support columns
that give it a space-age quality.
*5600 Biscayne Boulevard, 33137
+1 305 762 5751
andiamopizzamiami.com*

Bacardi Buildings, Midtown
Raise the bar

The Bacardi Tower is one of those
buildings that you pass and then
immediately want to know more
about. Though the front of the
high-rise is unremarkable, the
tiled murals that bookend it stand
out. The former HQ of Bacardi
was designed by Cuban architect
Enrique Gutierrez in 1963 and the
tiles were made by Brazilian artist
Francisco Brennand.

The Mimo building can also
be considered Latin American in
its materials and style. And the
colourful 1973 annex built by
Ignacio Carrera-Justiz, known
colloquially as the "Jewel Box",
is equally interesting.
2100 Biscayne Boulevard, 33137

Mi-what?

Miami modern, or Mimo
(pronounced My-mo), is the
Magic City's sunny offshoot of
mid-century modern. Notable
examples can be found along
Biscayne Boulevard and
Miami Beach; look out for the
Fontainebleau Hotel and the
North Beach Bandshell if you
want more of a hit.

Neon Miami
Glow ahead

①
Mac's Club Deuce, South Beach
Dealer's choice

The neon sign at this bar – which claims to be the oldest drinking den in Miami, dating back to 1926 – is the real deal. Located in South Beach and owned by gruff Second World War veteran Mac Klein, this place is both an absolute dive and a genuine institution.

The sign has changed little since it was put up although Klein has added a personal touch – he's been the proprietor since 1964, after all – with a proud neon "Mac's" above "Club Deuce". And why the name? It's at number 222 – and a two is also known as a deuce.
222 14th Street, 33139
+1 305 531 6200
macsclubdeuce.com

②
New Yorker Hotel, Mimo District
Sign of the times

We love this sign; somehow it manages to be classic and a little seedy at the same time (which is how Miami can sometimes feel – in the best possible way, of course). The neon belongs to a characteristic motel on a strip of mid-century buildings on Biscayne Boulevard.

The building is an original from the 1950s and has been a part of the Figueroa family for more than 30 years (the owner's father, a Cuban exile, bought the property in 1980). The hotel was refurbished in 2009 and is the area's first boutique offering.
6500 Biscayne Boulevard, 33138
+1 305 759 5823
hotelnewyorkermiami.com

③
Coppertone sign, Mimo District
Bum deal

Coppertone is a US producer of suncream established in the 1940s. Its most iconic foray into the world of neon was with a 1958 advertisement – featuring the Coppertone girl – made by Tropicalites (the same company behind the original Vagabond sign).

The sign was returned to its original site at Biscayne Boulevard in 2008 after briefly adorning the nearby Concord Building in the 1990s. It belongs to the Biscayne Mimo Association but Coppertone's parent company has helped out: when the group couldn't afford liability insurance, it stepped in to save the day.
7300 Biscayne Boulevard, 33138

④
Miracle Theatre, Coral Gables
Show stopper

Constructed as a cinema in 1948, this mid-century beauty was originally run as a single-screen venue that was operated by media company Wometco. The City of Coral Gables then acquired the Miracle Theatre in 1995 and it became the home of theatre company Actors' Playhouse, which has continued to draw a crowd ever since.

Despite the change in use the original neon marquee – with its distinctive external spire and "Miracle" lettering – has remained, fully restored a couple of years ago.
280 Miracle Mile, 33134
+1 305 444 9293
actorsplayhouse.org

Generation gap

Miami has much to protect that is significant. We're glad there's been investment in the timber houses of the South River Drive Historic District; it would be great to see the graffiti-covered Marine Stadium Grandstand re-envisioned too.

①
Mediterranean revival,
Coral Gables
Something borrowed

Nowhere is Mediterranean revival
such a hodge-podge of styles than
in Miami, borrowing heavily as it
does from Italy and Spain. Indeed,
the style is often just referred to
as "eclectic" here in a bid to get
round this conundrum. Revival
architecture abounds in Miami,
from the much-publicised Versace
Mansion to the residential houses
of the Buena Vista neighbourhood.

One of the classics is Douglas
Entrance in leafy Coral Gables (a
planned community dating back
to the 1920s). The terracotta-tiled
entrance was designed by the area's
main architect, and proponent
of the City Beautiful Movement,
Phineas Paist.
Douglas Entrance, Douglas Road,
33134

Eclectic taste
—
Revival
architecture
abounds
in Miami

②

Neoclassical, Riverside
Floral tribute

With all the art deco, Mediterranean revival and Mimo architecture on show, the neoclassical style gets less attention in Miami (maybe it doesn't quite go with the palms). The JW Warner House, however, is one such magnificent example. The house is named after the man who established the Miami Floral Company in 1906. Six years later he had this home designed by George Pfeiffer and it was the residence of the Warner family (and the office of the floral company) until the 1970s. The standout features are the Ionian columns, Palladian window and porte-cochère.
111 Southwest 5th Avenue, 33130

New leaf

Urban development and hurricanes have reduced Miami's greenery; an initiative from Miami-Dade County is looking to increase the area's tree canopy from 14 to 30 per cent by 2020, thanks to the planting of one million trees.

Top talent: Craig Robins

Craig Robins (*see page 74*) has been behind some of the city's most important developments in the past three decades. Despite his law background, he became involved in the art-and-design scene after he graduated. He was one of the principal investors in South Beach in the 1980s, a time when its art deco buildings were falling into disrepair and the area was both rundown and dismissed as a glorified retirement home (dubbed "god's waiting room"). Robins helped spur Miami's renaissance through the renovation of these buildings.

In the 1990s Robins turned his attention to the City of Miami mainland and the dilapidated Design District. He set about first attracting designers and studios and then expanding his rejuvenation concept to include retail. As well as having an expansive private art collection that is open to the public, he has been one of the major players behind Art Basel Miami Beach and the subsequent creation of Design Miami, both of which have helped the city get away from its sun-and-sand cliché and compete as a major international cultural hub.

③
Arts and Crafts, Little Havana
Singular storey

The Arts and Crafts movement
may have originated in the UK
and continental Europe in the late
19th century but it arrived in the
US in the early 1900s, determined
to bring good taste back to design
in all its forms.

In architectural design, the
movement's ideals were often
manifested in the form of
bungalows. The single-storey
structures were big on natural
materials such as wood and were
made to be affordable – ensuring
that even those of modest means
could enjoy decent architecture as
part of their every day.

The building on 16th Avenue
is a well-preserved example of a
1920s Belvedere Bungalow, with
wide eaves, a deep-set porch and
windows arranged to maximise
natural cross-ventilation – no
bad thing in the Miami heat. The
oolitic limestone is also a very
Miami touch.

138 Northwest 16th Avenue, 33125

④
Central Hall, Little Havana
Building blocks

The Riverview Historic District –
the eastern part of Little Havana
– was rapidly developed in the
1920s and 1930s, when a large
Jewish population moved to the
area, attracted by the weather and
business opportunities.

It was during this period that
the classic Central Hall buildings
were produced – essentially
walk-up apartment blocks in
Mediterranean and Mission styles.
The area, which became known as
Little Havana in the 1960s with the
first wave of post-revolutionary
Cuban migration, is full of these
buildings. This example on South
West 5th Street is a classic.
1069 Southwest 5th Street, 33130

Centre stage

OK, so Central Hall is a bit of
a sub-genre. The architectural
style can vary but it is such
an iconic form of building in
Little Havana that we deemed
it worthy of inclusion. These
are walk-up apartments,
typically flat-roofed and with
ornamentation around the very
top of the façade.

If you want to talk good design we should credit the work these braces are doing

⑤
Wood-frame vernacular,
Downtown
Echoes of old Miami

None of the nearby architecture is anything like this wooden-framed house from about 1897, which was originally one of 30 homes built by railroad magnate Henry M Flagler for workers developing his Royal Palm Hotel.

Palm Cottage, the last surviving example, was saved and moved to this Downtown location in 1980. There are few other timber houses in Miami except in the South River Drive Historic District, which has six buildings that were completed before 1915. They include the River Inn, being conserved by Vagabond owner Avra Jain.
60-64 Southeast 4th Street, 33131

Projects to watch

01 Miami Worldcenter, Downtown: A huge chunk of land in Downtown – 11 hectares to be exact – is slated to become the home of this mixed-use project that will include retail, hospitality and residential elements. The most interesting element is a new high-speed rail terminal planned for 2017, All Aboard Florida, which will link Downtown with West Palm Beach.
miamiworldcenter.com

02 Shore Club, Miami Beach: This Collins Avenue hotel is set to be refurbished during 2016 under the ownership of HFZ Capital, with bigger rooms (but fewer of them) and an added condo dimension to come. Brazilian architect and designer Isay Weinfeld will be sprinkling his stardust over the whole project.
hfzcap.com

03 The Underline, Brickell: Inspired by New York's High Line, Miami's Underline will transform a seldom used strip of land under Miami's Metrorail line into a 16km linear park. The project starts at the Miami River, north of the Brickell Metrorail station, and runs to Dadeland South Station. The park will include native plants and two paths: one for pedestrians and the other for cyclists.
theunderline.org

I'm Miami's official photographer. I just haven't told Miami yet

①
Mark Newson fence,
Design District
Division belle

The fence that borders the Design and Architecture High School, fashioned in 2007 by London-based Marc Newson, is no ordinary structure. It consists of a metal frame of 400 vertical fins, so that it shifts in appearance depending on how it's viewed.
4016 Northeast 2nd Avenue, 33137
miamidesigndistrict.net

②
Bus shelters, Little Havana
Shady character

These tile-roofed stands sprinkled around Southeast 8th Street (which locals call Calle Ocho) were originally bus stops. Some still fulfill that purpose but others simply provide shade. The decades of maintenance they have received – not least as part of the Calle Ocho Improvement Project – is testament to their status as heritage pieces.
Southeast 8th Street, 33135

③
Manhole covers, Miami Beach
Underground scenes

Manholes can be unsightly and utilitarian at best but in Miami Beach there has been an attempt to bring beauty to these functional objects. Artist Garren Owens drew up a design in cast iron that was rolled out in 2007, tapping into art deco style with central themes of the ocean and sun.
Prime example in the New World Center park at 500 17th Street, 33139

Design museums
Cool and collected

The Freedom Tower is a distinctive feature on Miami's skyline

②
Coral Gables Museum,
Coral Gables
Urban exploration

Housed in two buildings, this museum covers the history of this wealthy neighbourhood that sprang up in the 1920s with a particular focus on urban design and architecture and their interplay with larger national and international themes. The space, opened in 2011, has nine exhibition galleries.

One of the structures is a former police and fire station from 1939, a blend of Depression moderne and Mediterranean revival that is worth a visit in its own right. The museum is shut on Mondays.
285 Aragon Avenue, 33134
+1 305 603 8067
coralgablesmuseum.org

①
MDC Museum of Art + Design,
Downtown
Towering reputation

The 17-storey Freedom Tower at Miami Dade College is one of Miami's most striking historic buildings. As a museum of art and design it's the place to see works by Joseph Beuys and Emilio Sanchez but it's also an architectural gem with a significant tale to tell.

Built in 1925 by New York architectural firm Schultze & Weaver to house the *Miami News*, this edifice modelled after the bell tower of the Cathedral of Seville became a focus for Cuban migrants during the Cold War.
600 Biscayne Boulevard, 33132
+1 305 237 7700
mdcmoad.org

Around the world in Coral Gables

Coral Gables developer George Merrick enlisted Mott Schmidt to come up with a series of themed villages spanning French Normandy, Cape Dutch and China. Today the houses are highly desirable properties.
coralgables.com

❸

Vizcaya Museum and Gardens,
Coconut Grove
Italian stallion

Everything about this Italianate
mansion, from the interiors to the
very Venetian boat mooring at the
back, yearns to recreate old-world
European sophistication. Finished
in 1916, the house was the winter
home of international harvester
James Deering, whose reputation
for opulence is borne out here.

Highly modern for its time, the
house had central-heating and
telephones but was designed to
look far older than it actually is.
Wander around the interior and
the vast central courtyard (now
covered with glass to allow it to be
air-conditioned) and marvel at the
French-inspired music room or the
Italian Renaissance dining room.
The landscaped gardens – which
are particularly popular for
quinceañera photo shoots – are
also not to be missed.
*3251 South Miami Avenue, 33129
+1 305 250 9133
vizcaya.org*

Stiltsville
Go out on a limb

Originally built as fishing outposts, a handful of shacks were set up in the middle of the sea – several miles from Downtown – back in the 1920s and 1930s. With prohibition, many turned into drinking and gambling dens.

Nowadays only seven houses remain, all built on stilts (hence the name) in order to survive hurricane season. The owners have become caretakers of their own homes, now part of a federal national park, and it's possible to spend a day on one of the colourfully painted timber constructions spotting dolphins and eyeing far-off skyscrapers.

Stiltsville residents continue to talk about Jimmy Ellenburg, who used to welcome Miami mayor LeRoy Collins to his home in the 1950s. Then there's the still-functioning Miami Springs Power Boat Club (*pictured, left*). The name Stiltsville caught on after Hurricane Betsy in 1965; before then the houses had been closer to the water. The most beautiful of the remaining houses has to be Gail and Antoinette Baldwin's the Baldwin Sessions House (*living room pictured*).
stiltsvilletrust.org

119

Sport and fitness
—— Deep impact

Thanks to Miami's ever-sunny climate, it often feels there are more bikini-clad beach dwellers than suited office workers. So if you need to get your beach body sharpish, we have the pick of the city's air-conditioned fitness spots for you to hone those biceps. Of course, it would be silly not to also take advantage of the balmy climate and head outdoors, even in the heat of summer. Choice beaches to work on your tan? We've got them covered. Likewise, where to head for the best windsurfing experience and where to pound the ground on a running route.

When it really gets too blistering outside (or if a hurricane hits), we've also included some interesting indoor options to keep fit Miami-style – and many of them are not your usual suspects. So slap on some sunscreen, grab those shades and get moving.

①
The Fontainebleau, Mid-Beach
Gold standard

This pool attained its iconic status when it appeared in the 1959 Frank Sinatra film *A Hole in the Head* and, five years later, the James Bond classic *Goldfinger*. A behemoth on the luxury outdoor scene, the complex is large enough to warrant the term "poolscape", as dubbed by The Fontainebleau's staff.

Grassy strips dotted with chairs lie between the collection of pools, while the more secluded cabanas offer butler service, refrigerators and TVs. Non-guests can rent a cabana for the day starting at $250.
4441 Collins Avenue, 33140
+1 305 535 2000
fontainebleau.com

Got to fly,
I have a
date with
a sun-
lounger

②
The Setai, South Beach
Infinite possibilities

Guests and visitors to The Setai are welcome to swim in the lap of luxury with a spa package. The complex boasts three infinity pools, each with a different feel, including an option for lap-swimmers, recreational dippers and families.

Tailored so guests can dive in year-round, the three pools have their temperatures precisely calibrated at 23.9C, 29.4C and 35C. The outermost, shaded by palm fronds and beach umbrellas, peers out to the Atlantic. With these warm waters and beach views, the cooler months are no reason not to visit.
2001 Collins Avenue, 33139
+1 305 520 6000
thesetaihotel.com

❸
Mondrian, South Beach
Out of sight

Swimming pools in Miami are more than just a hotel afterthought and this is one of our favourites. Dutch designer Marcel Wanders has created a beautifully curved pool with uninterrupted views of Biscayne Bay and Downtown.

A labyrinth of padded sun-loungers surrounds the pool, with hammocks hanging in the nearby garden, all of which fill up during Sunday parties with resident DJs on the decks. If you're not a guest, a meal at the restaurant will gain you poolside access throughout the week.
1100 West Avenue, 33139
+1 305 514 1500
morganshotelgroup.com

Four beaches

01 North Shore Open Space Park, North Beach: Located far from the madding crowds on Ocean Drive, this beach is flanked by a lush green park. Visitors are welcome to walk their four-legged friends in the enclosed dog-park – but not on the beach – and runners can use the paved pathways for a picturesque jog that boasts spectacular views of the Atlantic Ocean.
miamiandbeaches.com

02 Matheson Hammock Park Beach, Coral Gables: A hidden gem tucked away in the southern fringes of the mainland, Matheson owes its distinct circular shape to the architects who built this artificial lagoon back in 1930.
miamidade.gov

03 Virginia Key Beach Park, Virginia Key: Virginia Key Beach Park opened in 1945 but closed in the 1980s. Saved from private development by a citizens' group, today this nearly 2km stretch of beach is accessible via the Rickenbacker Causeway and boasts a verdant backdrop to the usual sea and sand.
virginiakeybeachpark.net

04 Bill Baggs Cape Beach, Key Biscayne: Wade through the warm clear waters along the shoreline of Bill Baggs Cape Beach and arrive at the lighthouse at the end, a historic monument dating back to 1825. This is one of the best vantage points in Miami to take in unobstructed ocean panoramas.
floridastateparks.org

Vagabond life
—
The pool has been restored to its 1950s glory

(4)
Venetian Pool, Coral Gables
Freshen up

This public pool offers stone accents and Mediterranean-inspired surroundings for the aquatically inclined. Opened in 1924 by developer George Merrick, the pool emerged from its previous life as a coral-rock quarry to become an iconic swimming spot for locals.

During the busier summer months the sizeable pool is drained every night and refilled with fresh water from up to 22 metres below ground; only low doses of chlorine are needed. This old-timer also features quaint towers and an arched bridge for spectators.
2701 De Soto Boulevard, 33134
+1 305 460 5306
coralgables.com

5 The Vagabond Hotel, Mimo District
Place to roam

Just beyond the mid-century charm of the roadside sign marking your arrival – and past the charismatic welcome in the hotel lobby – lies the rectangular pool of The Vagabond. While it's not the most luxurious option on our list, the oversized sun-loungers are nestled poolside among the impressively restored exteriors, lending a stylish 1950s feel.

A day-pass gets you in the charming pool decorated with mermaid and dolphin mosaics. Lovingly refurbished in 2014, the pattern was constructed using tiles salvaged from the original hotel.
7301 Biscayne Boulevard, 33138
+1 305 400 8420
thevagabondhotel.com

Water sports/activities
Find the action

(1)
Paddle-boarding, Miami Beach
Swept away

It may look peaceful – with
silhouettes stood upright on their
boards drawing strokes on the water
with a single paddle – but this is a
full-body workout.

"Most of the core muscle groups
are engaged," says Mike Hirooka,
paddle-boarding instructor at
The Standard (*see page 18*). He
teaches beginners how to navigate
the currents while maintaining
their control and balance in the
calm waters surrounding the hotel;
if you're lucky you might even see
the dolphins and manatees that
often visit the area.
40 Island Avenue, 33139
+1 305 673 1717
standardhotels.com/miami/spa

(2)
Surfing, Haulover Beach
Nude tubes

Although its fame stems from being
clothing-optional, Haulover Beach
– north of Bal Harbour – also
receives some of the most vigorous
waves in Miami during the surfing
season between October and April.
Unfortunately, Haulover doesn't
have any rental shops offering
surfboards so visitors have to drop
by the Liquid Tube Surf Shop to
get one for a day on the ocean.
The family-owned business has
been providing surfboards and
other water-activity equipment
for rent, as well as surfing lessons,
since 2004.
10800 Collins Avenue, 33154
+1 305 947 3525
miamidade.gov; liquidtube.com

Flamingo Park

Close to Ocean Drive,
Flamingo Park was created
in 1950 and now includes an
aquatics centre, football pitch
and comprehensive line-up
of athletic amenities. It also
has 17 well-lit tennis courts
and an American-football
stadium. The aquatics centre
has a temperature-controlled
eight-lane lap pool that is
maintained at a delightfully
particular 27.8C throughout
the year.

Dog-owners can bring their
pets to the bark park; there's
also a children's playground.
Renovated in 2013, the park's
track, tennis and team-sport
facilities have been upgraded
to serve every fitness need.
miamibeachfl.gov/
parksandrecreation

③
Windsurfing, Virginia Key
It's a breeze

Along the Rickenbacker Causeway, between the mainland and Key Biscayne, lies Hobie Island Beach Park, christened Windsurfer Beach because it's hands-down the best part of Miami for it. Long stretches of shallow water make it safe even for the most amateur surfers.

"Windsurfing is a sport that keeps challenging you whether you've learnt it for an hour or have been doing it for 10 years," says Ovidio DeLeon, whose company Sailboards Miami offers lessons whatever your standard, along with rental services.
1 Rickenbacker Causeway, 33149
+1 305 892 8992
sailboardsmiami.com

Energy free

There are parks scattered across Miami and most are fitted with outdoor training gyms and volleyball courts (dubbed Fitness Zones by the city). They are a fun and free way for people to keep hale and healthy.

④
Jet-skiing, South Beach
The hot seat

"From South Pointe you have ocean access, bay access and all the famous sights of Miami within 15 minutes on a jet ski," says Adam Burnett, manager of American Watersports from his perch overlooking the Meloy Channel in South Pointe. The firm provides jet-ski-guided tours ranging from one to two hours, skimming past landmarks such as Star Island, Monument Island, Bayside Miami and Fisher Island. If you'd prefer to explore on your own, they also offer the largest riding area in South Beach.
300 Alton Road, Pier A, 33139
+1 305 538 7549
jetskiz.com

⑤
Kayaking, North Beach
Trail off

Covering more than 422 hectares of forest, water and mangroves, Oleta River State Park is Florida's largest urban park. It's a 30-minute drive or so from Downtown and the northern section of the park provides a scenic kayaking experience courtesy of the Oleta River. Row around the mangrove swamps on a canoe or a kayak; you can rent from the Blue Moon Outdoor Center. The company also runs various tours, including an atmospheric adventure lit by the glow of the full moon.
3400 Northeast 163rd Street, 33160
+1 305 957 3040
bluemoonoutdoor.com

Beach sports

01 **Volleyball, South Beach:** While you can find courts for Miami's unofficial beach sport in almost every park in the city, there's no question that beach volleyball is best played on the seaside. South Beach Volley is a group of like-minded players who have taken it upon themselves to maintain the courts on 8th Street and Ocean Drive. There's a strict no-reservation policy so the courts are available for anyone who wants to turn up and play.
southbeachvolley.com

02 **Ultimate Frisbee, South Beach:** Slowly gaining popularity in Miami is the fast-paced game that involves people diving for flying discs. Every Friday evening at 18.30 a casual, non-competitive pick-up game of ultimate frisbee is held at the 14th Street lifeguard kiosk in South Beach.
sflultimate.com

Yes, I'm fine thanks. Just resting

Indoor options
Sweat shops

(1)
RedBike Studios, Brickell
Stay tuned

Miami resident Albert Ghitis founded RedBike Studios in 2014 to fill a gap he saw in the city. "I wanted to make a workout that didn't feel like exercise," he says. "We pedal to the beat of music, adding full-body choreography."

His indoor cycling facility in Brickell is fitted with Schwinn AC Sport Cycle Trainers and most sessions last 45 minutes. Two in-house nutritionists are available to advise on dietary needs and you can replenish after class at the RedBoost smoothie bar with a juice and well-deserved açai bowl.
1399 Southwest 1st Avenue, 33130
+1 305 646 1499
redbikestudios.com

(2)
Barre Motion Miami, South Beach
Assume the position

A form of exercise that is gaining popularity in Miami, barre motion borrows moves and postures from ballet, yoga and pilates. "There is no other form of exercise that combines strength, flexibility, balance and mindfulness as intensely," says founder Julie Jacko.

You don't need to be a pro or even that nimble; Jacko promises everyone will work up a sweat at her Signature Motion class. Participants, she says, can look forward to "lean, long, sexy bodies" within weeks of joining. Sign us up.
1560 Lenox Avenue, Suite 103A, 33139
+1 305 534 8087
barremotionmiami.com

(3)
5th Street Gym, South Beach
Sting like a bee

In 2009, boxing trainer Dino Spencer came across a piece of history: the then defunct 5th Street Gym, where Muhammad Ali used to train. Spencer contacted original owner and Ali's former cornerman Angelo Dundee and partnered with him to revive the gym a year later.

Today a diverse clientele ranges from professional athletes to supermodels. Visitors can buy a day pass or sign up for individual lessons, with facilities including a boxing ring and personal-training equipment.
1434 Alton Road, 33139
+1 305 763 8110
5thstgym.com

Gyms

01 Anatomy at 1220, Mid-Beach: Anatomy at 1220 entered Miami's fitness scene in 2014, promising a more holistic and premium alternative to the available offerings in the market.
anatomyat1220.com

02 Equinox, citywide: With three locations across Miami (South Beach, Brickell and Coral Gables), New York's Equinox has outfitted Miami with state-of-the-art fitness equipment and unparalleled amenities. As with all Equinox outposts, gym users can expect toiletries by Kiehl's and eucalyptus-infused towels.
equinox.com

Tennis
At your service

Tennis courts

01 Cranden Park Tennis Center, Key Biscayne: Every spring, Crandon Park Tennis Center plays host to the 12-day Miami Open tournament on Key Biscayne. It has 26 courts in total, including six clay and two grass courts. Seven remain open after sunset and players can also have their racquets restrung here.
cliffdrysdale.com

02 Tropical Park Tennis Center, Olympia Heights: Located on the southwestern side of Miami, the Tropical Park Tennis Center has 12 floodlit tennis courts. It also has outdoor racquetball courts that can be reserved in advance. Slightly out of the way, the courts are impeccably maintained and worth the drive.
tropicalparktennis.com

Whew!
I'm one
roasted
bird

Bouncing back

Billed as the world's fastest sport, 'jai-alai' originated in Spain during the late 18th century. The game is played on a three-walled court and resembles squash. Miami 'jai-alai' is one of the few places left to watch a match.
jai-alai.info/miami-jai-alai.html

Cycling routes
Wheels of fortune

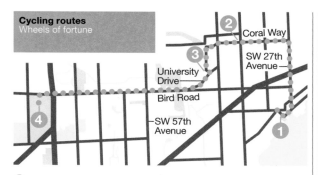

Coral Way
Ⓞ
SW 27th
Avenue
Ⓞ
University
Drive
Bird Road
SW 57th
Avenue
Ⓞ
Ⓞ

① Coconut Grove and Coral Gables
Tour of duty

Miami's bike culture is still in its nascent phase and most residents continue to depend on their cars to get from A to B. But hopefully, with the continued expansion of the Citi Bike bikeshare programme on both sides of Biscayne Bay, more people will be willing to switch.

In the meantime, the lively residential neighbourhoods of Coconut Grove and Coral Gables are best explored on bicycle. After picking up a Citi Bike at the corner of Grand Avenue and McFarlane Road, start at ① *Peacock Park* and continue in a general northerly direction until you hit Coral Way and turn left. This is Coral Gables' Miracle Mile, which is lined with a bevy of interesting retail options and ends at the ② *Coral Gables City Hall*, built in the Mediterranean revival style. Cycle south on Segovia Street past the ③ *Coral Gables War Memorial Youth Center*, which was opened in 1945. Continue southwest on University Drive, cross the stream on Bird Road and cycle straight until ④ *Tropical Park*, adjacent to the Bird Road Art District. Visit citibikemiami.com to find a convenient docking station.

STARTING POINT: Peacock Park, 2820 McFarlane Road, 33133

② Virginia Key
Passing traffic

Nature-loving cyclists tired of having to look over their shoulders for cars will be pleased with what

Virginia Key has to offer. Tucked between the mainland and Key Biscayne, the northern tip of the island features numerous mountain bike routes (the North Point Trails), all clearly signposted and offering degrees of difficulty; start with the easiest and go from there. Enjoy the shade of the trees and unsullied views of the Miami skyline, Fisher Island and Port of Miami. The trails owe their existence to the Virginia Key Bicycle Club, which convinced city-planners to allow them to convert the former dumping ground into cycle tracks.

STARTING POINT:
Arthur Lamb Jr Road, 33149

NOTE: Trails are colour-coded according to difficulty and wearing a helmet is mandatory.

Norris Cut

Virginia Key
Mountain
Bike Park

Haircare and grooming

01 Thierry Mas, Sunset Harbour: With more than two decades of experience styling hair, Thierry Mas started his salon in 2004 in the residential Miami Beach neighbourhood of Sunset Harbour. It is now known for its attentive customer service as much as its good taste.
thierrymas.com

02 Well Groomed Gentleman, Coral Gables: Established in 2014, Well Groomed Gentleman has updated the classic barbershop for modern times. Besides haircuts and shaves it also offers massages, shoe-shining and facials.
wellgroomedgentleman. com

03 Churchill's Barbershop, Downtown: Gents fit snugly into red leather seats at Churchill Barber Shop in Downtown for a cut and shave. The shop also stocks up on grooming essentials such as pomades and shaving oils.
+1 305 379 8615

04 Salon Vaso, South Beach: Both men and women can enjoy the hairstyling services of Vaso Spirou in the comfort of antique barber chairs that sit on hardwood floors. This South Beach salon is located just two blocks south of Lincoln Road.
salonvaso.com

I wonder if hair scissors can be applied to trimming ties

Running routes
Hit your stride

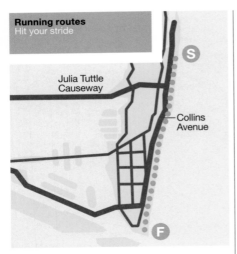

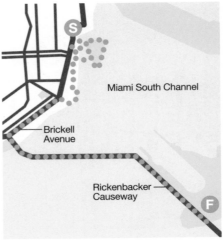

1

South Beach and Miami Beach Boardwalk
Life and sole

DISTANCE: 6.2km
GRADIENT: Mostly flat
DIFFICULTY: Easy
HIGHLIGHT: The varied architecture, ranging from art
   deco and Mimo to Mediterranean revival
BEST TIME: Weekday mornings

There is nothing complicated about this run, which covers the whole southeastern flank of Miami Beach. It's a great way to survey the area's iconic architectural landscape on one side, along with ocean views on the other, without having to dwell among the bustle of tourists on Ocean Drive.

Begin at the Indian Beach Park at Collins Avenue, which marks the start of the Miami Beach boardwalk. After a warm-up, take the wooden pathway and follow it south. Thanks to conservation efforts – which have included the planting of greenery such as palm, coconut and sea-grape trees – the run is a cool and shady one. Very quickly you'll pass the famous Fontainebleau Hotel to your right. Keep going, using the openings to the beach to alternate between the sand and the boardwalk whenever you feel in the mood for a bit more of a challenge. Stop in at one of the pavilions for a rest if the need arises.

When you hit 23rd Street the wooden planks become pavement. In 2012 the boardwalk received $1m for upgrading works, with segments converted to pavement to make them more wheelchair accessible. The historic art deco district starts a little further down; Miami's most rambunctious strip is offset a little by Lummus Park, which you run through before emerging at the other end at South Pointe. The finishing point is a relatively quieter spot to catch your breath – and hail a cab to make your way back.

2

Brickell to Virginia Key
Crowd control

DISTANCE: 10km
GRADIENT: Undulating in parts
DIFFICULTY: Hard
HIGHLIGHT: View of the city from the top of
   Rickenbacker Causeway
BEST TIME: Early morning before rush hour

Adjacent to the Downtown core, Brickell is one of Miami's densest neighbourhoods, populated as much by office blocks and residential condominiums as it is people. If you're in town for business it's likely you'll find yourself in one of the hotels in the area. Thankfully the waterfront is a quick jog away.

Starting at Brickell Point, an archaeological site at the mouth of the Miami River believed to be 2,000 years old, run south along the River Walk Trail. You'll have to nip right along Brickell Park Path and then back left again after a block to resume running by the water. Take the Brickell Key Drive Bridge when you reach it; it takes you to the manmade island of Brickell Key. Created during the late 19th century, it is now a private development and the location of the Mandarin Oriental. Jog around the periphery and back to the mainland. Hang a left along Brickell Bay Drive, which ends at Southeast 15th Road. Turn left on Brickell Avenue and continue towards Brickell Hammock.

Just before hitting Alice Wainwright Park, turn left and scale the second bridge of the run. The William M Powell Bridge spans more than 1km and reaches nearly 24 metres in height. Take a quick breather at the apex and watch the sailboats before continuing downhill onto the Rickenbacker Causeway and Virginia Key. From here it's a quick walk to the Rusty Pelican at the tip of Rickenbacker Marina. After a full meal, you might want to call a taxi for the ride back.

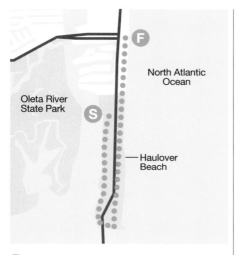

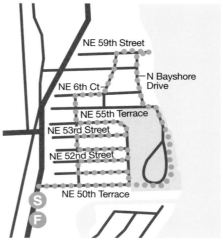

③
Haulover Beach
With the grain

DISTANCE: 5.5km
GRADIENT: Mostly flat
DIFFICULTY: Moderate
HIGHLIGHT: View of the ocean from Newport Fishing Pier
BEST TIME: Late afternoon

A short drive north of Bal Harbour on Collins Avenue, Haulover Park is a 40-hectare sandbank that was opened shortly after the Second World War in 1948. Today six tennis courts, a marina and a golf course share the land with carefree beachgoers on the clothing-optional northern tip of Haulover Beach (*see page 122*). This route wraps around the southern section of the isle, offering views of Oleta River State Park to the west and the Atlantic Ocean to the east.

Haulover Beach has two main car parks; start your jog at the smaller one further north (if you drive you should also park here). Keeping right, you'll pass a tiny inlet where you'll see yachts docked. Jog along the western side past the Haulover Marine Center. Across the water is Oleta River State Park. Press southwards, passing the tennis courts, and quickly nip in and out of the south car park. You'll encounter a larger harbour with more vessels docked. Keep tracing the water margins, looping around the base of the islet and crossing Collins Avenue towards the eastern part of Haulover. This side is where the beaches are: either run north along Atlantic Way (watch out for traffic) or the beach.

Leave behind Haulover and continue north towards Sunny Isles Beach. Run past the parade of condominiums, ending your run at Pier Park. Don't miss the chance to walk onto the Newport Fishing Pier for some spectacular ocean views.

④
Morningside Park
Home stretch

DISTANCE: 5.1km
GRADIENT: Flat
DIFFICULTY: Easy
HIGHLIGHT: The preserved residences here are mostly built in the Mediterranean revival style
BEST TIME: Afternoon, beneath the shady trees

The most residential of the routes listed here, Morningside Park is tucked away in a private but accessible neighbourhood of the same name in the Upper East Side. While this run takes you through the park, it also brings you around the single-family homes that were constructed in the Mediterranean revival during the 1920s and 1930s.

This run starts at Northeast 50th Terrace, passing the friendly sentry post and heading towards the park up ahead. Upon entry take the outermost trail, which curves right to border Biscayne Bay. This waterfront park is dotted with stately old banyan trees. Exiting the park north, take North Bayshore Drive until Northeast 59th Street. Tuck right and loop around the traffic island and run back westwards. Turn left on Northeast 6th Court and admire the residences. Many of these abodes have only one or two floors and the majority of them sport tiled roofs: a hallmark of the Mediterranean revival style. Morningside is one of only a handful of historically preserved residential areas in Miami; the streets are tree-lined, providing shade and making it easy to run at any time of day.

When you're done exploring Morningside, head back the same way you came and end your run back at the mouth of Biscayne Boulevard and Northeast 50th Terrace. There are a couple of cafés and restaurants just across the street for a thirst quencher before heading back.

Walks
—— Find your
own Miami

There are two things you need to know about Miami (and we're talking about Miami-Dade County here, that wonderfully confusing amalgamation that includes the Miami mainland, Miami Beach and places such as Coral Gables). Firstly, get beyond the beach. Secondly, yes, the car may rule but there are plenty of walkable places to discover – you just have to know where.

NEIGHBOURHOOD 01
Coral Gables
Pretty green

Oh Coral Gables, you leafy wonder, you planned little oasis you. This neighbourhood is testament to the boom of the 1920s when a young Miami was full of speculators, property magnates and eccentric personalities from the north who had come to make their fortunes. Out of this beautiful chaos came something rather ordered: the planned community of Coral Gables, the brainchild of a certain George Edgar Merrick. Like other neighbourhoods (Buena Vista being one), "the Gables" is heavily influenced by Mediterranean revival architecture, essentially an eclectic mishmash of styles that borrows heavily from Spain and Italy.

Coral Gables is technically (less so in reality) a separate city, part of the Miami-Dade County – a straight shot south from Downtown and Brickell past Coconut Grove. You pass shady street after shady street to get here and Coral Gables has a certain debonair, refined quality; it feels quietly wealthy and old world but, like much of the city, has a Latin edge thanks to the Cubans, Colombians and Venezuelans that have settled here.

When you walk around you'll find that everything is contained within a couple of streets. That includes the cringefully named Miracle Mile, once (and to a certain extent still) a mecca for Latina brides-to-be looking for wedding dresses and currently undergoing regeneration.

Culture circles
Coral Gables walk

Kick your neighbourhood walk off at the **❶** *Coral Gables Museum*. Here you can kill two birds with one stone: get some cultural insight and tour an interesting building (it's a former police and fire station built in 1939). Facing away from the museum, turn right and walk to Salzedo Street. Turn right and continue two blocks to Alhambra Circle. On your left at the intersection, you'll see the old-school **❷** *Café Demetrio*, a building from the

Getting there

The Metrorail connects Miami International Airport, Downtown and Coral Gables, among other destinations. The City of Coral Gables also has its own free trolley that meets with the Metrorail and heads down Ponce de Leon Boulevard, stopping every few blocks.

1920s. It's a good stop for a sweet treat and caffeine fix. Then cross Salzedo Street and head east on Alhambra Circle, crossing Ponce de Leon Boulevard, and continue until you reach the impressive triangular-shaped office building 121 Alhambra Plaza. At the base is Argentinian restaurant ③ *Siga La Vaca*, which does a roaring trade in all things beef.

If cow isn't your thing, worry not: you can eat at ④ *La Palma* instead. You reach it by going around the northern side of 121 Alhambra Plaza (if you're standing near the obelisk water feature and facing the building, head to the left) and walking up Alhambra Circle to the interesection of Galiano Street. Turn right and the entrance to the restaurant will be immediately to your left. La Palma, an Italian-inspired restaurant with a great outdoor patio, is a prime example of Mediterranean revival – it was designed in 1924 by George Merrick's cousin H. George Fink. Follow Galiano Street around the bend and then turn right back onto Alhambra Plaza. Retrace your steps for two blocks before turning right

back onto Salzedo Street. After one block, turn left onto Alcazar Avenue and on your right, next to a juice bar, you'll see ⑤ *Jimmy's Barber Shop*, worth a chop (note: it's cash-only). Keep going on Alcazar and when you hit Southwest 42nd Avenue, turn left. Head south, crossing Alhambra Circle, Giralda Avenue and Aragon Avenue. When you reach the major intersection at Coral Way, you'll see to your far right the magnificent ⑥ *Coral Gables City Hall* with its Corinthian colonnade – a 1928 building on the National Register of Historic Places.

Retrace your steps along Southwest 42nd Avenue to Aragon Avenue and turn right. Cross Salzedo Street and just past the museum you'll come to the excellent ⑦ *Books & Books*, which has a great selection of magazines and an outdoor bar. Keep going a little further, and on the same side of the road you'll find ⑧ *Peterbrooke Chocolatier* (try the chocolate-covered popcorn).

Three doors down you'll find refreshments at ⑨ *Small Tea*. It's a remarkably technical café with an automated temperature and "agitation" system for each brew – and there are almost 100 to choose from.

Continue along and you'll reach home-interiors hotspot ⑩ *Aragon 101*. Then hang a right onto Galiano Street and take the first right again onto the aforementioned, ahem, Miracle Mile. If you've timed your walk well you can catch an evening play at ⑪ *Miracle Theatre*, a mid-century modern former cinema. If you're keen to finish it all off with a beverage or a latin-inspired meal, turn back up Salzedo Street and walk half a block to ⑫ *Bread + Butter*.

Address book

01 Coral Gables Museum
285 Aragon Avenue, 33134
+1 305 603 8067
coralgablesmuseum.org

02 Café Demetrio
300 Alhambra Circle, 33134
+1 305 448 4949
cafedemetrio.com

03 Siga La Vaca
121 Alhambra Plaza, 33134
+1 305 448 2511
sigalavaca.com

04 La Palma
116 Alhambra Circle, 33134
+1 305 445 8777
lapalmarestaurant.net

05 Jimmy's Barber Shop
303 Alcazar Avenue, 33134
+1 305 448 9235

06 Coral Gables City Hall
405 Biltmore Way, 33134
+1 305 446 6800
coralgables.com

07 Books & Books
265 Aragon Avenue, 33134
+1 305 442 4408
booksandbooks.com

08 Peterbrooke Chocolatier
227 Aragon Avenue, 33134
+1 305 446 3131
peterbrookecoralgables.com

09 Small Tea
205 Aragon Avenue, 33134
+1 786 401 7189
smallteaco.com

10 Aragon 101
101 Aragon Avenue, 33134
+1 305 443 7335
aragon101.com

11 Miracle Theatre
280 Miracle Mile, 33134
+1 305 444 9293
actorsplayhouse.org

12 Bread + Butter
2330 Salzedo Street, 33134
+1 305 442 9622
breadandbuttercounter.com

NEIGHBOURHOOD 02

Design District and Buena Vista
Reclaiming past glories

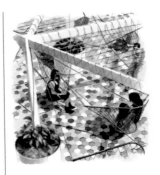

Buena Vista began its existence as a pineapple plantation in 1892. Three decades later, ornate estates were built ranging from Mediterranean revival to art deco and masonry vernacular. At the same time, a few blocks south, the Design District (which historically belonged to leafy Buena Vista) began taking shape as furniture sellers settled during the city's land boom. Yet as Miami entered its darker, crime-ridden days it fell into urban decay and even Buena Vista wasn't its splendid self any more. That changed from the 1990s when property mogul Craig Robins began rejuvenating the area. Soon, historic structures such as the iconic Moore Building from 1921 were revamped, while new masterpieces from the likes of architect Sou Fujimoto were constructed. This attracted designers and luxury brands, transforming it into a place where public art, architecture, fashion, design and gastronomy meet.

Even though Buena Vista and the Design District couldn't be more different, they harmonise to form a rare (for Miami, anyway) pedestrian-friendly destination, ideal for a Sunday stroll. Thanks to landscape designer Nathan Browning's efforts, the Design District's streets are lined with flourishing indigenous trees that offer some much-needed shade and may one day rival Buena Vista's green canopy – a pretty hard act to follow.

Food, fashion and fine art
Design District and Buena Vista walk

Buena Vista and the Design District lie between Miami Beach and Miami International Airport (a 15-minute drive each way). It's simple to catch the Miami Trolley to the area from Biscayne Boulevard in Downtown. If you have a car, park in the Palm Court Parking Garage (enter via Northeast 38th Street).

Exit the car park through Buckminster Fuller's ❶ *Fly's Eye Dome*, a spherical model of Fuller's 1977 "autonomous dwelling machine" prototype. Once in open-air Palm Court, check out French artist Xavier Veilhan's Le Corbusier fibreglass sculpture and the hand-painted-glass façade by Japanese architect Sou Fujimoto on the building that houses ❷ *Hublot*, alongside other boutiques.

Next, head across the court to restaurant ❸ *Ella*, named after restaurateur Michael Schwartz's eldest daughter, and pick up a homemade lemonade and a rock-shrimp roll to enjoy while swinging on ❹ *Konstantin Grcic's Netscape*, a 24-seat web of hanging chairs.

Once you've had a little break, walk west along Northeast 39th Street. It's Miami's Champs-Élysées, where luxury labels including Louis Vuitton, Dior, Valentino, Tom Ford, Marc by Marc Jacobs and Givenchy all have artfully designed shops. Over the rooftops you'll spot two enormous billboards portraying beach scenes by conceptual artist John Baldessari; titled *Fun* they are on the façade of the City View Garage. Continue west, past the historic ❺ *Buena Vista Post Office* and turn

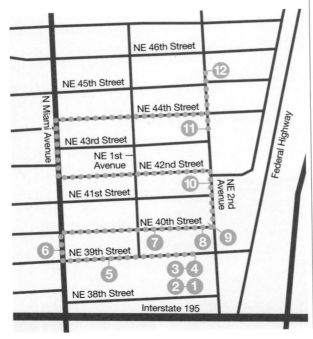

right on North Miami Avenue. Here you'll find ⑥ *Swampspace*, artist Oliver Sanchez's showroom, worth popping into for frequent musical and artistic performances.

Turn right onto Northeast 40th Street for some window-shopping. It's worth visiting ⑦ *Markowicz Fine Art*, a pulsating gallery that exhibits Andy Warhol, Keith Haring, Damien Hirst and Tom Wesselmann. Further down the road, drop into Parisian concept store ⑧ *Maison Margiela*, which offers menswear and womenswear, accessories, shoes and stationery.

On the opposite side of the street you'll spot the ⑨ *Moore Building*, the imposing atrium which sets the stage for Zaha Hadid's dynamic *Elastika* installation. Also be sure to cross Northeast 2nd Avenue and walk along Marc Newson's Dash Fence. This 30-metre installation surrounding Miami's Design & Architecture Senior High School is made of 400 metal blades, creating a wave pattern that alters depending on your point of view.

Before leaving the Design District and entering Buena Vista, it's time for a rest: head north on Northeast 2nd Avenue and just after the intersection of Northeast 41st Street you'll

see ⑩ *Eména Spa*. After a Swedish massage, turn left onto Northeast 42nd Street and see the scenery shift from storefronts to eclectic homes and tropical gardens.

Amble on lanes overhung with palm, mango and royal poinciana trees and marvel at the homes built from coral rock. Especially noteworthy is the Interamerican Institute for Democracy at the corner of North Miami Avenue. Turn right and don't miss the art deco residential building further north at number 4400, with its nautical porthole windows and music-note stairs.

Once the sun sets, head east on Northeast 43rd Street to Northeast 2nd Avenue. Turn right and take a seat in the idyllic courtyard of Mediterranean restaurant ⑪ *Mandolin Aegean Bistro* on 2nd Avenue. Its whitewashed walls, blue doors and delicious seafood will transport you to the Greek islands in no time. For dessert, visit ⑫ *Buena Vista Chocolate & Wine* a couple of blocks north for pralines handmade by eighth-generation chocolatier Claude Postel.

Getting there

The Biscayne Route on the free Miami-Dade Trolley services the Design District before looping around and heading south. It travels west on Northwest 39th Street and turns left onto North Miami Avenue. It runs 06.30 to 23.00, Monday to Saturday.

Address book

01 Fly's Eye Dome
140 Northeast 39th Street, 33137

02 Hublot
140 Northeast 39th Street, Suite 103, 33137
+1 786 762 2929
hublot.com

03 Ella
140 Northeast 39th Street, Unit 136, 33137
+1 786 534 8177
ellapop.me

04 Konstantin Grcic's Netscape
140 Northeast 39th Street, 2nd Floor Terrace, 33137

05 Buena Vista Post Office
66 Northeast 39th Street, 33137
usps.com

06 Swampspace
3940 North Miami Avenue, 33137
swampspace.blogspot.com

07 Markowicz Fine Art
110 Northeast 40th Street, 33137
+1 305 308 6398
markowiczfineart.com

08 Maison Margiela
3930 Northeast 2nd Avenue, Suite 101, 33137
+1 786 718 1931
maisonmargiela.com

09 Moore Building
191 Northeast 40th Street, 33137
+1 305 722 7100
bridgehouseevents.com

10 Eména Spa
4100 Northeast 2nd Avenue, Suite 301, 33137
+1 305 438 3777
emenaspa.com

11 Mandolin Aegean Bistro
4312 Northeast 2nd Avenue, 33137
+1 305 749 9140
mandolinmiami.com

12 Buena Vista Chocolate & Wine
4512 Northeast 2nd Avenue, 33137
+1 305 396 6056
buenavistachocolate.com

NEIGHBOURHOOD 03
North Beach
The alternative

Being overshadowed by its rambunctious sister in the south has been a good thing for North Beach, which retains a small-town feel amid its 500 or so architecturally significant buildings. Not to be confused with North Miami Beach on the mainland, this neighbourhood extends from 63rd Street to 87th Terrace and part of it was included in the National Register of Historic Places in 2009.

It boasts the city's highest concentration of Mimo buildings, along with a sprinkling of art deco, streamline moderne and classical revival offerings. Until the 1930s, the area consisted primarily of swamplands, mangroves and little else; the bulk of the development was undertaken after the Second World War. Architects erected buildings that considered the area's tropical climate – these elements, such as exterior stairways, broad eaves and ventilation holes, persist to this day.

During the cold war, Jews fleeing Cuba also flocked here, infusing the area with its vibrant culture and cuisine. Of course, as with other parts of Miami, you don't have to look far to be able to see the Latin influence. While the area's retail landscape still has some way to go, its cultural and architectural heritage more than warrants a full day here. If you drive, parking is abundant compared to other parts of the city but make sure you don't lose track of time and forget to top up the meter.

Mimo and art deco
North Beach walk

Start your day by picking up a croissant and coffee at ❶ *Astrid & Stephanie* bakery, then cross Collins Avenue. To your right, you'll see the green eaves of the ❷ *Deauville Beach Resort*, one of the oldest buildings in the area. Besides being a handsome example of Mimo architecture (having been constructed in 1957 by Melvin Grossman), the grandiose hotel famously hosted The Beatles for a live broadcast of *The Ed Sullivan Show* in 1964. The likes of Frank Sinatra, Judy Garland and Sammy Davis Jr have also performed in these hallowed halls.

After checking out the grand lobby and pool, head north and turn left on 71st Street. Four blocks ahead is ❸ *O Cinema Miami Beach*,

housed in the former Byron Carlyle Theater, the original sign of which still remains thanks to conservation bylaws. Because it specialises in arthouse, foreign and experimental films – instead of blockbusters – this is the place to discover your new favourite director.

After you've caught a flick, turn left out of the cinema and walk to Dickens Avenue. Turn right and continue to the intersection of 75th Street where you will find ❹ *Temple Menorah*, the hub of the Jewish population here since the 1950s. The building of this community centre, school and place of worship, with its tower replete with ventilation holes, is a striking example of Mimo architecture.

For a literal taste of Jewish culture, turn right down 75th

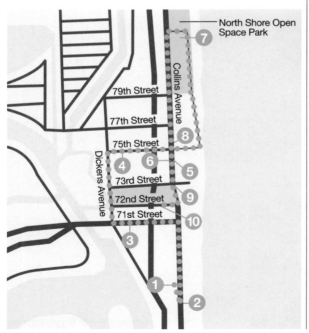

North Shore Open Space Park

7

Collins Avenue

79th Street

77th Street

75th Street **8**

Dickens Avenue

4 **6**
5
73rd Street

3

72nd Street **9**

71st Street **10**

1

2

Street, walk back to Collins Avenue and then turn right again. In half a block, grab a takeout brisket sandwich at ⑤ *Goldstein's Prime*, which has fed Jews and Gentiles for decades.

Across the street is an eye-catching specimen of art deco architecture. Although it is now a gym, the façade of ⑥ *Surf Theater*, with its wavy motifs and symmetry, has been left untouched. Residents flocked to it during the 1960s, when it was run by Miami-based cinema Wometco Enterprises.

Head back to 75th Street and turn right. Walk to the beach and turn left onto the Atlantic Way boardwalk. Head north, enjoying the ocean views while you amble towards the ⑦ *North Shore Open Space Park*. Spanning 78th Street to 87th Terrace, this is one of the rare patches of sand on Miami Beach where you don't have to endure the rows of hotels or condos that typically trace the seaside, making it a restful place to enjoy the sea breeze.

After some peace and quiet, make your way south along Collins Avenue. If the weather is too hot,

Getting there

Miami Beach's second trolley, the North Beach loop, was launched at the end of 2014. The free service (with onboard wi-fi) runs from 08.00 to midnight. It heads north on Collins Avenue, turns west on 88th and then south on Harding Avenue, before looping west and back around.

the ⑧ *North Shore Branch Library* on 75th Street will provide respite. The squat, functional structure, two blocks from the beach, offers the chance to browse the works of the many writers that have made this city their home.

Step back into sunlight and walk south until 72nd Street, the location of the ⑨ *North Beach Bandshell* built in 1961. A bronze memorial plaque marks the spot where North Beach's first building – the Biscayne House of Refuge – was built in 1875, when it served as a haven for shipwrecked sailors. The area was revamped in 2010 and consists of an outdoor amphitheatre that seats nearly 1,500 people. You might even catch a performance in one of the outdoor courts.

By now you'll be starting to hear your stomach rumbling. Turn right onto 72nd Street and walk one block to ⑩ *George's Italian Restaurant & Lounge*, owned by siblings George and Elizabeth Iglesias. Everything served, including the pasta, bread and pizzas – plus the rather good limoncello – is freshly made. Not a bad way to round things off.

Address book

01 Astrid & Stephanie
6772 Collins Avenue, 33141
+1 305 397 8680
astridandstephaniebakery.com

02 Deauville Beach Resort Miami
6701 Collins Avenue, 33141
+1 305 865 8511
deauvillebeachresortmiami.com

03 O Cinema Miami Beach
500 71st Street, 33141
+1 786 207 1919
o-cinema.org

04 Temple Menorah
620 75th Street, 33141
+1 305 866 2156
templemenorahmiami.org

05 Goldstein's Prime
7419 Collins Avenue, 33141
+1 305 865 4981
goldsteinsprime.com

06 Surf Theater
7420 Collins Avenue, 33141

07 North Shore Open Space Park
78th Street to 87th Terrace, 33141

08 North Shore Branch Library
7501 Collins Avenue, 33141
+1 305 864 5392
mdpls.org

09 North Beach Bandshell
7275 Collins Avenue, 33141
+1 305 672 5202
northbeachbandshell.org

10 George's Italian Restaurant & Lounge
300 72nd Street, 33141
+1 305 864 5586
georgesmiamibeach.com

NEIGHBOURHOOD 04
South Beach
Escape the tourist traps

South Beach may be the best-known neighbourhood in Miami; indeed, often out-of-towners forget that anything exists beyond this bubble. It's here that the sea, the sand, the pastel colours and the architecture that have made this tropical oasis famous come together in sweet harmony – but it wasn't always this way.

Miami Beach began life as a piece of land for planting and harvesting coconuts. By 1913, two men – John Collins and Carl Fisher – became partners and developed the mangroves lining the shore into oceanfront; the subsequent 1920s boom saw 800 art deco structures erected, many of them now preserved. The area's big regeneration drive started in the early 1980s and today the progress is evident in the sparkling hotels (and a healthy smattering of tourists) lining Collins Avenue and Ocean Drive.

There are some true architectural and cultural gems in South Beach so be sure to look out for them on your walk. It's also vital to head off on a few detours to indulge in some lighter fare, which should incorporate the enjoyment of a few cocktails. Granted, a walk here may involve dodging a dawdling tourist or reveller from time to time but that certainly shouldn't deter you from visiting. And the best news is that if you start proceedings around midday, you can drag this one out into the wee hours of the morning.

The late one
South Beach walk

The first stop on this walk is Miami's top bookshop **1** *Books & Books* at its Lincoln Road location. We recommend a visit here to pick up a few periodicals or some new fiction, which will come in handy for the next stop on the walk. If you don't find any suitable reading material, pop to **2** *Base* next door and have a gander at its fine selection of print; this menswear shop also has magazines and art books.

Take your reading materials and head towards Jefferson Avenue, where a left turn will bring you to 17th Street. Turn right and continue to the centre that houses the **3** *New World Symphony*, which was designed by Frank Gehry. The adjoining Soundscape Park is ideal for a leisurely stroll: winding paths weave under aluminium pergolas that are strewn with bougainvillea vines. The structures, designed by Dutch landscape-architecture firm West 8, are intended to resemble cumulus clouds.

Afterwards, exit onto 17th Street and walk east towards Washington Avenue where, on the left side of the street, you will soon be faced by the **4** *Temple Emanu-El Synagogue*. This is the oldest conservative temple in Miami, having been built in 1948. The striking building mixes Byzantine and Moorish architectural styles and is topped with a copper dome.

By now you will have worked up enough of an appetite to walk to **5** *Taquiza*. To get there, follow Washington Avenue south, passing the park again on your right, then

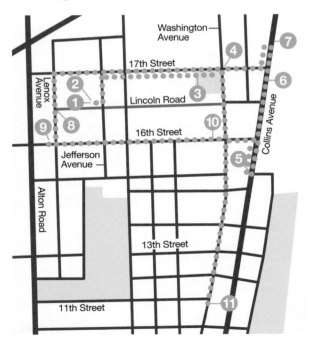

turn left on 16th Street and right
on Collins. There, near the corner
of 15th Street, you'll find some of
the best street food in Miami: the
taco stand is *the* place for handmade
tortillas. Hang around in its shady
courtyard then head north on
Collins towards ⑥ *National Hotel*,
which will appear on your right.
Walk into the lobby of this recently
restored 1939 building in order to
see one of the best collections of
original art deco lighting in Miami.

Continue on Collins to ⑦ *The
Raleigh* hotel where, on the right
side of the lobby, you will find its
charming coffee bar. Perch at the
counter on one of its mounted
stools for a brief reprieve with a
flat white. Once you're sufficiently
caffeinated, head one block south
to 17th Street, and turn right. Walk
west until you reach Lenox Avenue,
and then turn left.

At the Lincoln Road intersection
you'll find the ⑧ *Colony Theatre*.
Built in 1935, it once served as a
Paramount cinema but today, after
years of renovation, it is a venue
for music, dance, theatre, opera,
comedy and film. You can walk in

to admire the renovation or make a
note of upcoming shows.

Now continue on Lenox until
you reach 16th Street, where a right
turn will bring you to ⑨ *SuViche*,
a Japanese sushi and Peruvian
restaurant. We recommend having
one (or a few) of the signature
pisco sours before heading to ⑩ *Do
Not Sit on the Furniture* by walking
east on 16th Street to Washington
Avenue. This dimly lit dancehall
says it all with its name: don't come
here to rest. It is known for its
themed music evenings so be sure
to check the line-up in advance and
come with the right footwear.

It may be well into the morning
by the time you leave so if you
have danced to the point of
working up an appetite, walk to
the ⑪ *11th Street Diner* by turning
right on Washington Avenue and
walking south to 11th Street. This
diner car lived in Pennsylvania for
44 years but was moved to Miami
in 1992; it's now one of the best
preserved art deco buildings on
South Beach. It's open 24 hours
so get cosy in a booth and start
the recovery.

Getting there

The South Beach Local bus
(Route 23) costs $0.25 and
departs every 20 minutes
or so. Its circuit of the entire
Sobe area starts at 20th Street
and West Avenue; it heads
south along Washington
Avenue and back up on
West Avenue, stopping every
couple of blocks.

Address book

01 Books & Books
927 Lincoln Road,
33139
+1 305 532 3222
booksandbooks.com

02 Base
927 Lincoln Road,
33139
+1 305 531 4982
baseworld.com

03 New World Symphony
500 17th Street, 33139
+1 305 673 3330
nws.edu

04 Temple Emanu-El
Synagogue
1701 Washington Avenue,
33139
+1 305 538 2503
tesobe.org

05 Taquiza
1506 Collins Avenue,
33139
+1 305 748 6099
taquizamiami.com

06 National Hotel
1677 Collins Avenue,
33139
+1 305 532 2311
nationalhotel.com

07 The Raleigh
1775 Collins Avenue,
33139
+1 305 534 6300
raleighhotel.com

08 Colony Theatre
1040 Lincoln Road,
33139
+1 305 674 1040
*colonytheatremiamibeach.
com*

09 SuViche
1119 16th Street,
33139
+1 305 777 3555
suviche.com

10 Do Not Sit on the
Furniture
423 16th Street, 33139
+1 510 551 5067

11 11th Street Diner
1065 Washington Avenue,
33139
+1 305 534 6373
eleventhstreetdiner.com

NEIGHBOURHOOD 05
Wynwood
Peaceful promenade

Wynwood is one of Miami's most easily walkable areas. Maybe it has something to do with its recent regeneration but you can wander around here and not feel like you're in the middle of a highway, which can be the case in some other parts of town. Despite it being easy to drive or get a taxi to pretty much anywhere else (beach included), Wynwood retains a tranquil feel.

A formerly run-down and at times no-go area, it has been transformed into a thriving arts district of contemporary galleries and street graffiti. But beyond the art there are also a growing number of decent restaurants – Coyo Taco may just be our favourite – alongside some decent retail offerings.

Everything is located in a small radius and on just a few streets, meaning you'd have trouble getting lost. With all the change going on – and that includes new businesses springing up all the time – it's hard to believe there was a riot here in 1990, after a police officer was acquitted in a fatal shooting. Times are changing. Wynwood takes after Bushwick, the Brooklyn neighbourhood in New York. Both are former Latino working-class and industrial areas that are now attracting creatives. But Bushwick is a little grittier; the sun, the palm trees and the clean streets make Wynwood Miami's tropical delight.

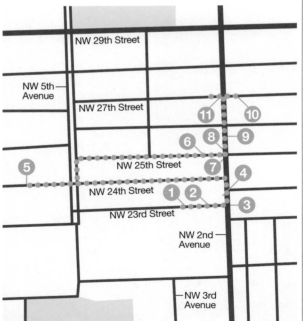

Rejuvenating experience
Wynwood walk

Get your vehicle of choice to drop you on Northwest 2nd Avenue and Northwest 23rd Street. Walk west on Northwest 23rd Street and on the right-hand side you'll come to ❶ *Hausammann Gallery*, a street-art exhibition space that has a second venue in Italy and a roster of international graffiti artists.

Heading back to Northwest 2nd Avenue you'll pass ❷ *Jan Kath Company* on the same side. The space is impressive, showcasing the German carpet-designer's work. His carpets – Persian tradition meets street art – are bizarre but fascinating in their ambition.

After a quick ogle, return to Northwest 2nd Avenue and turn left. On the right next to the Robert Fontaine Gallery, you'll see ❸ *Basico*. If new in town you'll be in need of Miami-appropriate – read colourful – clothing; the swimwear here is a winner.

After some retail therapy, head across the street to ❹ *Coyo Taco*. This place does beautifully presented tacos on an aesthetically pleasing metal rack, though bear in mind that you'll be having lunch later. It's also a lively evening spot: there's a speakeasy-style club through the door at the back.

Next it's time for a drink; Wynwood has become a hub for microbreweries. Facing north, head left on Northwest 24th Street to ❺ *Wynwood Brewing Company*. You need to keep going for a few blocks, past apartment buildings and a rather nasty-looking bar called Shots. It begins to feel a bit industrial but persevere: in-between Northwest 5th

HAUSAMMANN GALLERY

Address book

01 Hausammann Gallery
251 Northwest 23rd Street,
33127
+1 305 924 1560
hausammanngallery.com

02 Jan Kath Company
221 Northwest 23rd Street,
33127
+1 786 558 4334
jan-kath.com

03 Basico
2347 Northwest 2nd
Avenue, 33127
+1 786 360 3688
shopbasico.com

04 Coyo Taco
2300 Northwest 2nd
Avenue, 33127
+1 305 573 8228
coyotaco.com

05 Wynwood Brewing
Company
565 Northwest 24th Street,
33127
+1 305 982 8732
wynwoodbrewing.com

06 Warby Parker
215 Northwest 25th Street,
33127
+1 786 605 1112
warbyparker.com

07 Pan American Art Projects
2450 Northwest 2nd
Avenue, 33127
+1 305 573 2400
panamericanart.com

08 Joey's
2506 Northwest 2nd
Avenue, 33127
+1 305 438 0488
joeyswynwood.com

09 Mmmm
2519 Northwest 2nd
Avenue, 33127
+1 786 703 3409
mmmmwynwood.com

10 Foldway
188 Northwest 27th Street,
33127
+1 786 452 7706
foldway.com

11 Alejandra Von Hartz
Gallery
2630 Northwest 2nd
Avenue, 33127
+1 305 438 0220
alejandravonhartz.net

Getting there

You can travel to and from this district using the free Miami-Dade Trolley service (Biscayne Route), which runs approximately every 15 minutes. It stops by Roberto Clemente Park. Operating hours are 06.30 to 23.00, Monday to Saturday, and 08.00 to 20.00 on Sunday.

and Northwest 6th avenues, you're there. Try the refreshing La Rubia – an American blonde beer – to cool off; the brewery also organises art tours of the area every second Saturday. Head back the way you came to Northwest 5th Avenue and turn left. Take the right turn onto Northwest 25th Street and keep going until just before you return to Northwest 2nd Avenue.

On your left you'll see eyewear specialist ⑥ *Warby Parker*. The shop is designed like a swimming pool (this *is* Miami, after all) and it sells floating key fobs, swimming caps and sunglasses. On the opposite side of the road, and keeping slightly erratic hours, is ⑦ *Pan American Art Projects*, a contemporary gallery that features mainly Latin American and Caribbean artists.

Turn left onto Northwest 2nd Avenue – north again – and immediately on your left you'll come to ⑧ *Joey's*, an Italian joint that gets packed at lunchtime so time your walk well. It was the first restaurant to open in a regenerated Wynwood back in 2008. If that doesn't take

your fancy, you can always try ⑨ *Mmmm* across the road. Yes, the name is tedious but we're big fans of the wallpaper, a copy of Beverly Hills Hotel's Martinique, and the menu is open-sandwich focused, perfect for a quick bite.

Keep heading north on Northwest 2nd Avenue, then swing right onto Northwest 27th Street and you'll see ⑩ *Foldway*. This nifty bike shop (specialising in fold-ups) is one of a new breed promoting pedalling in a city not known for it. They can also help organise graffiti tours at the weekend.

Return to Northwest 2nd Avenue and cross the street, staying on 27th. You'll come to the ⑪ *Alejandra Von Hartz Gallery*, promoting conceptual and contemporary art, as well as being another gallery with a big roster of Latin American artists. For a final pit-stop head around the corner south on Northwest 2nd Avenue to Wynwood Block, a shopping centre that offers Jucy Lu juices, Mister Block coffee shop and the Wynwood Letterpress for stationery lovers. Take your pick and reward yourself for a route well walked.

Resources
—— Inside knowledge

We've shared the best spots for you to experience Miami's sights and sounds, from seaside shopping to stone-crab shacks. Now it's only a question of finding your way around this car-centric city without a hitch, which is where this section will come in handy. It will also give you an overview of the annual events, the Spanglish slang that's becoming the lingua franca, the city's party tunes and the come-rain-or-shine activities to make your stay in the Magic City, well, magical.

Transport
Get around town

01 Car: This is really the only way to get around Miami. Join the Maserati-populated highways in a rental car – or better yet in a cab, as finding a parking spot feels a little like winning the lottery. If you're driving, download one of Miami's parking apps: PayByPhone (for the mainland) and Parkmobile (for Miami Beach).
miamiparking.com; miamibeachfl.gov

02 Trains: Miami is built on swampland so don't except a sophisticated subway system. But do expect a 23-station Metrorail available from Miami Airport to Dadeland in the south and Palmetto in the north, all for a standard fare of $2.25. It also connects you to downtown Miami's futuristic and free Metromover. The forthcoming All Aboard Florida will link Miami and Orlando.
miamidade.gov; allaboardflorida.com

03 Bus: The Metrobus covers the entire Miami-Dade County for $2.25 and there's also a retro trolley bus service (think a bus made to look like a tram) that takes passengers around mainland Miami for free. Both have a bicycle rack.
miamidade.gov

04 Bike: Citi Bike is Miami's bike-sharing system. Choose one of 1,000 bikes from over 100 stations for $4 per 30-minute period (the first 30 minutes are free) or $24 for a one-day pass.
citibikemiami.com

05 On foot: We'd love Miami to be more walkable but there are places where you have to drive, especially in the sultry summer. If you find a spot for a stroll, winter temperatures are more agreeable.

06 Boat: Opulent but the finest view by a mile. Try Y Charter.
ycharter.com

07 Flights: Miami International Airport (MIA) is 15 minutes from South Beach (although its signage is needlessly confusing); Fort Lauderdale-Hollywood International (FLL) is 40-60 minutes. Alternatively there are business airports nearby, including Miami Executive, Opa-Locka Executive and Homestead General.
miami-airport.com

Vocabulary
Local lingo

Miami is a bilingual city – the Spanish-speaking population outnumbers English speakers – so this could be of use.

01 The Beach/the Grove/the Gables/the Key: What locals call Miami Beach, Coconut Grove, Coral Gables, etc.
02 Bueno: Translates to "good" but can also mean "well".
03 Cafecito: The only coffee you should be drinking in Miami. This Cuban espresso is brewed from a dark roast and topped with *espuma*, a sugary foam.
04 Casa Yuca: A term used to describe someplace *very* far away: "I had to drive all the way to Casa Yuca to pick her up."
05 Chanx: The anglicisation of *chancleta* or flip-flop.
06 Dale: This could mean a number of things, from "Let's go" to "Come on".
07 Getty: A get-together or small party.
08 Key rat: A Key Biscayne resident who rarely leaves the neighbourhood.
09 Porfa: Please, you should know this. It's the shortened form of *por favor*.
10 Tiki-tiki music: Fast-paced house or techno.

Soundtrack to the city
Five top tunes

The following songs pay homage to Miami and capture the city's chilled Cuban and Latino vibe.

01 Will Smith, 'Miami': Who doesn't want to "party all day" in a place where every day is like Mardi Gras to this 1998 Whispers-sampling hit?

02 Miami Sound Machine, 'Conga': "Let the music move your feet" to this 1985 worldwide hit, sung by Cuban-born and Miami-based Gloria Estefan.

03 Betty Wright, 'Miami Groove': Wright's R&B-and disco-influenced records embodied the city during the *Miami Vice* era.

04 Blondie, 'The Tide is High': Miami-born Debbie Harry's seaside theme song.

05 Sam & Dave, 'Hold on, I'm Comin'': The Miami-based duo landed their first major hit with this R&B number in 1966.

Best events
What to see

01 Art Deco Weekend, Miami Beach: Initiated by the Miami Design Preservation League, this annual three-day event celebrates the nation's art deco gems.
January, artdecoweekend.com

02 Coconut Grove Arts Festival, Coconut Grove: A three-day gathering that occurs every Presidents' Day weekend, showcasing the work of more than 360 artists and craftsmen.
February, coconutgroveartsfest.com

03 Miami International Film Festival, citywide: This fantastic festival celebrates local and international films at venues across the city.
March, miamifilmfestival.com

04 Miami Open, Tennis Center at Crandon Park: Watch the world's best tennis players compete in the sunshine state (it has been dubbed the "winter Wimbledon").
March, miamiopen.com

05 Ultra Music Festival, Bayfront Park: Ultra brings together DJs and more than 150,000 electronic-music fans.
March, ultramusicfestival.com

06 O, Miami, citywide: This month-long annual festival aims to introduce poetry to everyone in Miami-Dade County and does so in the most creative ways.
April, omiami.org

07 Miami International Fashion Week, Miami Beach: Think spectacle and resort wear.
May, miamifashionweek.com

08 Miami Broward One Carnival, Miami-Dade County Fairgrounds: This parade and carnival enlivens the city the Sunday before Columbus Day.
October, miamibrowardcarnival.com

09 Miami Book Fair International, Downtown: This eight-day literary celebration dates back to 1984 and brings more than 450 authors and hundreds of publishers and booksellers to the city.
November, miamibookfair.com

10 Art Week, Miami Beach: The entire art world jets to Miami for its annual Art Week led by the prominent Art Basel Miami Beach. Other fairs include Design Miami and Nada.
December, artbasel.com; miamiandbeaches.com

Rainy day
Weather-proof activities

Miami days are seldom spoiled by rain showers but when it starts to pour, here's where we hide out.

01 Pérez Art Museum Miami (Pamm): You can easily spend the whole day inside Pamm's spacious galleries; after all, the museum has about 1,800 pieces in its collection.
pamm.org

02 The Spa at Mandarin Oriental: Situated on Brickell Key island, this three-storey spa and wellness centre is inspired by ancient Asian and Ayurvedic traditions. No matter what the weather is, you'll feel heavenly here after a Thai massage or soothing sauna session.
mandarinoriental.com

03 O Cinema, Wynwood: Sit out the storm in this 112-seat independent movie theatre. Not only is it a cinema, it's also an art gallery exhibiting local talent. If the mood takes you, an afternoon can be spent with some popcorn and a book from the film-themed library.
o-cinema.org

Sunny days
The great outdoors

With 249 days of sunshine per year, Miami was built for the outdoors; from seaside swims and sprints to rooftop pool siestas, there's no shortage of things to do. Here's what not to miss.

01 Catch a boat to Stiltsville: Forget the outside world for a day and head to Stiltsville in Biscayne National Park, a 1930-established "village" now comprising of seven wooden huts on stilts. You can rent a furnished house for the day ($50 per person); enjoy the panorama of Miami, spot some dolphins, drop a line to catch a fish or two and cool off in the turquoise waters.
stiltsvilletrust.org

02 Alfresco swim, shop and stroll: Visit Coral Gables – the "City Beautiful" – and head to the European gardens of the Vizcaya Museum or hang out at the municipal Venetian Pool to swim and sunbathe.
vizcaya.org; coralgables.com

03 Day trips: Cruise down the Overseas Highway until you reach the southernmost tip of the US, Key West. This historic island city (only 140km from Cuba) was the favoured holiday destination of Ernest Hemingway. If you'd rather enjoy the outdoors, drive to the Everglades National Park and spend the day among alligators, manatees and 366 species of chirping birds instead.
keywest.com; nps.gov

About Monocle
⎯⎯ Behind the curtain

London calling
⎯
Midori House is in Marylebone

In 2007, Monocle was launched as a monthly magazine briefing on global affairs, business, culture, design and much more. We believed there was a globally minded audience of readers that were hungry for opportunities and experiences beyond their national borders.

Today Monocle is a complete media brand with print, audio and online elements – not to mention our expanding network of shops and cafés. Besides our London HQ we have seven international bureaux in New York, Toronto, Istanbul, Singapore, Tokyo, Zürich and Hong Kong. We continue to grow and flourish and at our core is the simple belief that there will always be a place for a print brand that is committed to telling fresh stories and sending photographers on assignments. It's also a case of knowing that our success is all down to the readers, advertisers and collaborators who have supported us along the way.

① International bureaux
Boots on the ground

We have an HQ in London and also call upon firsthand reports from our contributors in more than 35 cities around the world. We also have seven international bureaux; for this travel guide, New York bureau chief Ed Stocker teamed up with Toronto deputy bureau chief Jason Li and MONOCLE writers Megan Billings and Marie-Sophie Schwarzer. They also used the help of Miami-based writers to ensure that we covered the best food, retail, hospitality and entertainment the city has to offer. The aim is to make you, the reader, feel like a local when you visit the Magic City.

② Print
Committed to the page

MONOCLE is published 10 times a year. We have stayed loyal to our belief in quality print with two new seasonal publications: THE FORECAST, packed with key insights into the year ahead, and THE ESCAPIST, our summer travel-minded magazine. To sign up visit *monocle.com/subscribe*. Since 2013 we have also been publishing books, like this one, in partnership with Gestalten.

Caffeine fix
—
Our London café is located on Chiltern Street

Radio
Sound approach

Monocle 24 is our round-the-clock radio station that was launched in 2011. It delivers global news and shows covering foreign affairs, urbanism, business, culture, food and drink, design and print media. When you find yourself in Miami you can listen to *The Daily*, which includes regular reports from our Toronto and New York bureaux and features interviews with a number of guests across the Americas region. We also have a playlist to accompany you day and night, regularly assisted by live sessions that are hosted at our Midori House headquarters in London's Marylebone.

Online
Digital delivery

We also have a dynamic website: *monocle.com*. As well as being the place to hear Monocle 24, we use the site to present our films, which are beautifully shot and edited by our in-house team and provide a fresh perspective on our stories. Check out the films celebrating the cities that make up our Travel Guide Series before you explore the rest of the site.

Retail and cafés
Good taste

Via our shops in Hong Kong, Toronto, New York, Tokyo, London and Singapore we sell products that cater to our readers' tastes and are produced in collaboration with brands we believe in. We also have cafés in Tokyo and London serving coffee and Japanese delicacies among other things – and we are set to expand this arm of our business.

Monocle
EDITOR IN CHIEF & CHAIRMAN
Tyler Brûlé
EDITOR
Andrew Tuck

**The Monocle Travel Guide
Series: Miami**
GUIDE EDITOR
Ed Stocker

ASSOCIATE EDITORS
Megan Billings
Jason Li
Marie-Sophie Schwarzer

DESIGNER
Jay Yeo

PHOTO EDITORS
Poppy Shibamoto
Renee Melides

PHOTO ASSISTANT
Shin Miura

PRODUCTION
Jacqueline Deacon
Dan Poole
Amy Richardson
Sonia Zhuravlyova
Chloë Ashby

Writers
Mikaela Aitken
Diliana Alexander
Antoinette Baldwin
Megan Billings
Robert Bound
Megan Cross Schmitt
Joey Edwards
Nelly Gocheva
Rob Goyanes
Liv Lewitschnik
Jason Li
Craig Robins
Marie-Sophie Schwarzer
P Scott Cunningham
Paul S George
Ed Stocker

Chief photographers
Andres Gonzalez
Brad Torchia

Still life
David Sykes

Images
Rui Dias-Aidos
Elvis Suarez
The Adrienne Arsht Center
for the Performing Arts of
Miami-Dade County

Illustrators
Satoshi Hashimoto
Tokuma
Hans Woody

Research
Mikaela Aitken
Melkon Charchoglyan
Joey Edwards
Eugenia Ellanskaya
Paige Reynolds
Matthew Singerman

Special thanks
Ashley Abess
Diliana Alexander
Paul Fairclough
Nelly Gocheva
Amanda Hale
John Lin
Timothy Lucraft
Adam Richmond
Craig Robins
Megan Cross Schmitt
Isha Suhag
Patrick Welch

A

Adrienne Arsht Center for the
   Performing Arts, *Downtown* 102
Alchemist, *South Beach* 48 – 49
Alejandra von Hartz, *Wynwood* 99
Allapattah 98
Alter, *Wynwood* 31
Andiamo (former General Tire
   Building), *Mimo District* 109
Apt 606, *Design District* 52
Arts and Crafts, *Little Havana* 113
Atrium, *South Beach* 49
Aubéry, *North Miami* 57

B

Bacardi Building, *Midtown* 109
Bal Harbour 31
Bal Harbour Shops,
   Miami Beach 59
Ball & Chain, *Little Havana* 46
Barre Motion Miami,
   South Beach 124
Base, *South Beach* 50
Beachcraft, *Mid-Beach* 39
Bentley Bay Condominiums,
   South Beach 107
Blue Collar, *Mimo District* 34
Books & Books, *Coral Gables* 62
Boxelder, *Wynwood* 47
Brickell 36, 124, 126
Brickell Key 26, 36
Broken Shaker at the Freehand,
   The, *Mid-Beach* 45
Buckminster Fuller's Fly's Eye
   Dome, *Design District* 108
Buena Vista 29, 130 – 131
Bus shelters, *Little Havana* 114

C

Casa Tua, *South Beach* 25, 41
Central Hall, *Little Havana* 113
City View Garage,
   Design District 107
Coconut Grove 116, 125
Coltorti, *South Beach* 50
Coppertone sign,
   Mimo District 110
Coral Gables 62, 92, 110, 111,
   115, 121, 125, 128
Coral Gables Art Cinema,
   Coral Gables 92
Coral Gables Museum,
   Coral Gables 115
Craig Robins Collection,
   Design District 96
Curve, *South Beach* 51
Cutler Bay 93

D

David Castillo, *South Beach* 97
David's, *South Beach* 42
De la Cruz Collection
   Contemporary Art Space,
   Design District 96
Delano, The, *South Beach* 24
Del Toro Shoes, *Wynwood* 61
Design District 32, 34, 49, 52,
   54, 55, 57, 58, 61, 95, 96, 107,
   108, 114, 130
Dina Mitrani Gallery, *Wynwood* 98
Dot Fiftyone Gallery,
   Wynwood 100
Downtown 52, 53, 58, 95, 97,
   100, 102, 114, 115
Drunken Dragon, *South Beach* 41

E

Eberjey, *South Beach* 60
11th Street Diner,
   South Beach 106
El Portal 57
En Avance, *Design District* 55
Enriqueta's, *Wynwood* 43
Essays 67 – 90
Essex House, The,
   South Beach 106

F

5th Street Gym, *South Beach* 124
Fillmore Miami Beach
   at Jackie Gleason Theater,
   The, *South Beach* 102
Fontainebleau, The,
   Mid-Beach 120
Fooq's, *Downtown* 40
4141 Design, *Design District* 57
Frangipani, *Wynwood* 56
Frankie, *Sunset Harbour* 53
Fredric Snitzer Gallery,
   Downtown 97

G

Gale, The, *South Beach* 27
Gallery Diet, *Wynwood* 98
Garcia's, *Miami River District* 28
Genius Jones, *Wynwood* 61
Gigi, *Midtown* 31
Glo, *El Portal* 57
Goldman Warehouse,
   Wynwood 92
Gramps, *Wynwood* 46
Grand Central Miami,
   Downtown 100

H

Harry's Pizzeria,
   Design District 32
Haulover Beach 122, 127
Hint, *Mimo District* 51
Holly Hunt, *Design District* 58

I

Institute of Contemporary Art,
   Miami, *Design District* 95
I On The District, *Design District* 61

J

Jet-skiing, *South Beach* 123
Joe's Stone Crab,
   South Beach 33

K

Kayaking, *North Beach* 123
Klima, *Mid-Beach* 38

L

La Mar, *Brickell* 36
Little Haiti 63
Little Havana 43, 46, 91, 113, 114
Locust Projects,
   Design District 99
Loewe, *Design District* 49
Lost Boy Dry Goods,
   Downtown 53
Lummus Park 104

M

Mac's Club Deuce,
   South Beach 110
Magazines 103
Makoto, *Bal Harbour* 31
Malaquita, *Wynwood* 56
Mandarin Oriental, *Brickell Key* 26
Mandolin, *Buena Vista* 29
Manhole cover, *Miami Beach* 114
Market at The Miami Beach
   Edition, *Mid-Beach* 30
Mark Newson fence, *Design
   District* 114
Martini Bar at The Raleigh,
   South Beach 44
MDC Museum of Art + Design,
   Downtown 115
Mediterranean revival,
   Coral Gables 111
Miami Beach 59, 114, 122, 126
Miami Beach Cinematheque,
   South Beach 92
Miami Beach Edition, The,
   Mid-Beach 22
Miami Light Project at Goldman
   Warehouse, *Wynwood* 92
Miami River District 28
Mid-Beach 18, 22, 30, 37, 38, 39,
   45, 120

Midtown 31, 109
Michael's Genuine,
    Design District 34
Mimo District 20, 32, 34, 51, 109,
    110, 121
Miracle Theatre, Coral Gables 110
Mondrian, South Beach 120
Monocle 140 – 141
Morningside Park, 127
Museum of Contemporary Art,
    North Miami 93

N

Naoe, Brickell Key 36
Nautilus, South Beach 19
Need to know 14 – 15
Neoclassical,
    Miami River District 112
Newsstands, citywide 103
New Theatre at the South Miami-
    Dade Cultural Arts Center,
    Cutler Bay 93
New World Center,
    South Beach 102
New Yorker Hotel, Mimo District 110
North Beach 123, 132
North Miami 57, 93

O

O Cinema, Wynwood 91
OFY, Downtown 52
Olympia Theater at Gusman
    Center, Downtown 100 – 101
1 Hotel South Beach,
    South Beach 21
1111 Lincoln Road,
    South Beach 108

P

Paddle-boarding,
    Miami Beach 122
Pamm Shop, Downtown 58
Park@420, South Beach 108
Pérez Art Museum Miami,
    Downtown 95
Plant the Future, Wynwood 60

R

Raleigh, The, South Beach 17
RedBike Studios, Brickell 124
Regent Cocktail Club, The,
    South Beach 44
Resources 138 – 139
Riverside 112
Royal Palm South Beach, The,
    South Beach 24
Rubell Family Collection,
    Wynwood 96

S

Sartorial Miami, Design District 54
Scottish Rite Temple,
    Lummus Park 104
Sebastien James,
    Design District 54
Setai, The, South Beach 120
Soho Beach House,
    Mid-Beach 18
South Beach 17, 18, 19, 21, 24,
    25, 27, 33, 35, 41, 42, 44, 49,
    50, 51, 55, 60, 92, 94, 95, 97,
    102, 105, 106, 107, 108, 110,
    120, 123, 124, 126, 134 – 135
Spinello Projects, Allapattah 98
Standard Spa, The,
    South Beach 18
Stiltsville 119
Sunset Harbour 53
Supply & Advise, Downtown 52
Surfing, Haulover Beach 122
Sweat Records, Little Haiti 63

T

Tap Tap, South Beach 35
Tower Theater, Little Havana 91
Tub Gallery Miami, Wynwood 99
27, Mid-Beach 37

U

United States Post Office,
    South Beach 105

V

Vagabond Hotel and Restaurant,
    The, Mimo District 20, 32,
    109, 121
Venetian Pool, Coral Gables 121
Versailles Restaurant, Little
    Havana 43
Virginia Key 123, 125, 126
Vizcaya Museum and Gardens,
    Coconut Grove 116

W

Webster, The, South Beach 50
Windsurfing, Virginia Key 123
Winter Haven, South Beach 106
Wolfsonian-FIU, South Beach 94
Wolfsonian shop, South Beach 55
Wood-frame vernacular,
    Downtown 114
Wynwood 31, 43, 46, 47, 56, 60,
    61, 91, 92, 96, 98, 99, 100,
    136 – 137
Wynwood Letterpress,
    Wynwood 60

We hope you have found the Monocle travel guide to Miami useful, inspiring and entertaining. There is plenty more to get your teeth into: our London, New York, Tokyo, Hong Kong, Madrid, Bangkok and Istanbul guides are on the shelves as we speak. And there's lots more to come. Cities are fun. Let's explore.

01
London
The sights, sounds and style of the British capital.

02
New York
From the bright neon lights to the moody jazz clubs of the US's starring city.

03
Tokyo
Japan's capital in all its energetic, enigmatic glory.

04
Hong Kong
Get down to business in this vibrant city of depth and drama.

05
Madrid
A captivating city that is abuzz with spirit and adventure.

06
Bangkok
Stimulate your senses with a mix of the exotic and eclectic.

07
Istanbul
Where Asia and Europe meet – with astonishing results.

08
Miami
We unpack the Magic City's box of tricks.